half-wheel

HELL

& *other cycling stories*

by Maynard Hershon

LIBRARY OF CONGRESS IN-PUBLICATION DATA
Hershon, Maynard.
Half-wheel hell & other cycling stories / by Maynard Hershon. p. cm.
ISBN: 1-884737-05-6
1. Bicycles — Humor. I. Title.
PN6162,H418   1996
813'.54 — dc20
96-18046
CIP

PRINTED IN THE U.S.A.
♻ PRINTED WITH RECYCLED PAPER

VELOPRESS
1830 N 55TH STREET
BOULDER, COLORADO 80301-2700
USA
303/440-0601 EXT17
303/444-6788 FAX
E-MAIL: velonews@aol.com

TO PURCHASE ADDITIONAL COPIES OF THIS BOOK
OR OTHER BOOKS FROM VELOPRESS,
CALL 800/234-8356
INT'L 303/440-0601 EXT 6

COVER PHOTO: COR VOS

Contents

I n 1983, as an adult returnee to college, I enrolled in a writing program at Dominican College, in San Rafael, California. I'd written a stack of papers, short stories and poems, but my writing didn't seem to be going anywhere. So I signed up for a journalism class called Writing For a Living. What an idea, I thought: the stuff of dreams, to write for your living. I didn't make any money in that class, but I did get to write, every week, and was graded with a thoroughness bordering on fanaticism.

There was no mystery to writing a successful piece for that class. A "style sheet" prescribed rules for punctuation, syntax, numerals, diet … everything about which one could wonder. The teacher demanded accurate editing. Otherwise, he applied red ink in astonishing amounts.

He forced us to do interviews, sometimes several a week, collecting quotes for our articles. He had no patience with excuses. He was very much "real world." We got the feeling that if we could please him with our writing we could please anyone.

While on his torture rack, I supported myself as a manager at a bike shop in Fairfax, California. One day, as they say, the phone rang. A gentleman from nearby San Francisco was starting a monthly free newspaper, to be called *California Bicyclist*. He was looking for writers, he said, to submit copy, especially copy about bicycle racing.

I told the gentleman that purely by accident he had reached the bicycle racing journalist of his dreams. Busy at work, I wrote down his number and, for several worthless reasons, failed to call him for a month.

When eventually I did recontact him, he seemed glad to hear from me and gave me (oh boy!) an assignment. He thought me worthy to cover the Coors Devil's Cup, an important weekend of racing not far away in Contra Costa county. He even promised me payment for my prose and photographic efforts.

Please understand that I would have paid *him* for the privilege of attending those races as "working press." Why, television and radio would be there, and correspondents from established bike magazines. And I would be there, too, shoulder to shoulder with famous bike-racing writers whose work I'd admired for years.

I covered those races. You could say, if you felt generous, that I did an okay job. I took pictures and interviewed famous racers, went home and wrote copy, and the magazine used it. I received in time a truly paltry sum of money.

But my name was in print. My name ... in print. I had a byline just like Art Hoppe. People came up and told me they liked my article. I felt set apart a little, as if maybe I knew something the bikie in the street did not know. After all, I had talked to John Howard.

Soon, I began to do a monthly results column for that paper including a paragraph or two of local racing news. I was then assigned the Nevada City Classic criterium, which I covered diligently and wrote about badly. I suffered my first ego deaths from severe editing. But I discovered that, even though I'd blotted my bluebook, I hadn't been expelled from school.

I continued my little column, kind of let down; perhaps I wasn't cut out for bicycle journalism after all. I had the tools, thanks to my writing teacher at Dominican. I had a camera, thanks to MasterCard. I had a little experience, thanks to *California Bicyclist*. I needed something more to step another rung up the bike-press ladder: I needed a connection.

Suddenly, my friend Owen Mulholland — who'd been writing about bike racing for years — asked me to call his editor at *Winning* magazine. That wonderful

Euro-style racing monthly was just one issue old.

Owen had been assigned a regular column, focusing on a fictitious bike shop, inspired by a series in an automotive magazine. The car mag's stories featured a kindly garage owner who helped troubled motorists in clever, memorable ways.

Owen had in fact submitted one article, which *Winning* ran — a fictionalized description of an ancient, revered San Francisco shop. Owen told me he doubted that he could come up with a story every month for the column. He thought maybe I could. Don't ask me why....

At that time, mind you, there was no fiction in any cycling publication. They ran technical articles detailing *ad nauseam* how things worked; touring articles about where or where not to ride; diet articles; and racing reports. No fiction or poetry.

I called *Winning*'s then editor Jack Simes, a famous former racer. He'd recently taken over the dormant U.S. Professional Racing Organization, and saw *Winning* magazine as the ideal platform to popularize pro cycling in this country. Jack told me he wanted a humorous, sentimental column about a bike store, a story that might make a reader more sympathetic with a shop owner or employee.

Having been just such an employee, I felt capable of writing the piece, and I did. It described a customer buying his first pair of racing shoes, and featured the dialogue between buyer and salesman, and the salesman's italicized thoughts.

I thought that the piece was somewhat funny and certainly sympathetic ... but it was not what Jack had in mind. Crushed but still determined, I wrote another article, focusing this time, on a real, historical racer, John Allis, whom I knew to be a buddy of the editor's. *Winning* took it ... and paid me a paltry sum of money. But who cared. I'd become, in that instant, the only published writer of bicycle fiction (non-fiction optional at writer's discretion) in the country.

I became a regular part of a national magazine I could be truly proud of. I became responsible for a page in the back of that magazine; a page that would be blank but for my invention.

I continued writing for *Winning* until 1993, when I moved on to start the "At the back" column for *VeloNews*, 18 times a year. And over the past five years, I've also contributed to every issue of my first-chance paper, *California Bicyclist* and *Texas Bicyclist*. This book is a compilation of 50 of the best stories I wrote for

Winning and the *California Bicyclist* and *Texas Bicyclist.*

• • •

Throughout, my editors have been super-supportive. If I called with a hare-brained article idea, my editor got excited as I was. "Sounds great! When can we have it?" Given such editorial encouragement, a writer can spread his or her wings and soar off the Plain of Ordinariness. He or she need never descend to the Twelve Energy Bar Comparison Test — my vision of cyclo-journalist hell.

Instead, that writer can reveal disappointment with a major parts maker, describing his sense of abandonment as if mourning a lost love. He can submit a lightweight column about saying hi to other cyclists and watch, wide-eyed, as it generates so much mail the postman is still in chiropractic care.

He can suggest that cyclists stay out of cars' way except where truly necessary — and provoke another storm of mail, making him aware of the charged, politicized nature of car-bike relations.

He can write about a nightmare bike shop customer. He can suggest to bike mag readers (who are more accustomed to food bar tests) that they practice random acts of kindness and senseless acts of beauty.

I find it difficult or impossible to write about things I'm not passionate about. I love the enthusiast press in all my activities. I love the lore, the history, the language, the legendary characters. I hope you do, too. Those passions serve me, maybe, as a kind of apprenticeship for my writing.

You may be thinking: That Maynard, what a life he's got, assembling a thousand words every few weeks. Serious money, trips to the Giro, to the DuPont, media-big shot status, free bike parts ... groupies probably. Why him and not me?

Because I know you feel that way, I'm gonna let you in on how this column business works. I'll tell you everything, all the secrets, every trick. Then — it'll be up to you. Italy beckons ... wake up and smell the espresso.

First mistake: You probably think you need a story idea. Take it from me, an idea can be helpful but it's not essential. For proof, next time you're in the checkout line at the supermarket, grab a magazine; doesn't matter which one. Let it fall open; read anything in there.

Honestly, do you think the writer had an idea, any idea, what he or she was writing about? Is that rag successful nonetheless? Oh my, yes. Start writing; don't wait until you have an idea.

But you do need structure. You should, experts say, start with a beginning, follow it with a middle, and end with an end. Thinking of your article that way makes writing easy.

My columns usually go like this: At the beginning, I tell you how wonderful things used to be. In the middle, I tell you things are no longer any good. At the end, I say they'll never be good again.

Three or four classic columns like that a year and I get trips to Italy. I'm eating prosciutto and melon in Milan, out of the sun under a Cinzano umbrella. You're home with the McNuggets and Hot Apple Pie. You drove through. Is that fair?

So, you take your idea, if any, and expand it into a beginning, middle and end. Use short sentences. Use words folks have heard before. Three syllables, no more.

Don't fuss about spelling and grammar; your editor will handle that stuff. Fussing will only smother your newborn creativity. Just get the piece written. Let someone else decide if "its" needs an apostrophe. Who cares, really? Is Arnold grammatical? Is Arnold making ends meet?

Once you've got the piece on paper, read it to yourself out loud to see if it flows well. If you can't read your handwriting get your third-grade teacher to help you. However you go about it, wait till you get home to read aloud to yourself; don't do it on public transportation. All the explaining will only smother your creativity.

Here's the true test: If you can read the whole piece to yourself without nodding off and losing your place more than twice — you've got yourself a *People* magazine article. If you fell asleep three to five times, don't despair: Mail the piece to your local all-sports monthly paper. More than five times, you're a lock for a mainstream bicycle mag feature article. Submit that manuscript, expect acceptance and party on. There's a novel lurking in you somewhere.

After acceptance comes editing. First, I fax my story to the editors. That way they have a hard copy that they can crumple up satisfyingly and hurl at the wastebasket. If they find something worth reading in all those words, we go over the good parts and try to make an article out of them.

Based on our phone discussions, I edit the story on my computer. Then my computer calls my publisher's and transmits the story. One or two more phone calls will usually fine-tune it to their and my satisfactions. It's as good as it's likely to get.

It'd be hard for me to write generally about life. I have found it easy (sometimes) and gratifying to write about bike riders. Almost by accident, some of the stories turn out to be full of life. I hope you think so, too.

Maynard Hershon
ALBANY, CALIFORNIA
AUGUST 1994

Session II
August 8 - 13, 1993
Beaver Creek® Resort

Maynard Hershon
Name

ON

RIDING

HALF-WHEEL HELL

Does the phrase "half-wheeling" sound familiar? No? Perhaps you haven't heard it, but I'll bet you've suffered from the practice.

Let's say you're riding with someone you've never ridden with before. You two are side-by-side on a sunny country road; no traffic disturbs the perfect tranquility. You pedal along and chat, a perfect Sunday morning.

You realize your friend has slipped maybe a foot-and-a-half in front of you; he's talking to you over his shoulder. You pick up your pace just slightly and pull even. He doesn't notice; the two of you never stop talking.

A minute later, it dawns on you that he's up there again, *half a wheel* ahead.

You think, uh oh, I'm lagging here, and you accelerate half-a-mile-per-hour and come up alongside. You ride next to each other a few yards; amazingly, magically, there he goes again, *half a wheel* ahead.

You can hardly tell how it happens. Are you slowing down? Is he picking up the pace momentarily?

Once more you mini-chase him down. As you do, you notice you're beginning to get irritated. As the miles pass by, again and again you find he has jumped half a wheel or half a bike length up the road.

You check your speedometer: You're *not* slowing down. He speeds up for an instant, long enough to gain *half a wheel*. He's traveling the same speed you are, only 18 inches ahead. You chase repeatedly; it's maddening, doing this.

The ride loses its sun-drenched contentedness. It's you against him, an undeclared, perhaps one-sided, silent struggle. The two of you smile and talk about everything but the cold war that you sense is escalating. Maybe, you think to yourself, he doesn't realize he's doing it.

So how can you blame him, you ask yourself, he doesn't know. He doesn't do it on purpose. He'll feel terrible if you complain. How can you say anything? He's such a good guy. But why would a good guy do this, over and over again?

Maybe he's stronger than you. That's it: He's used to riding that little bit faster. He's probably reining himself in today on your account, but he can't help straining a little at the bit. You're the problem after all. You're holding him back.

You abruptly realize you're feeling sorry for yourself. Out on your bicycle on a perfect road on a perfect day, riding with a perfectly nice person and you feel sorry for yourself.

It occurs to you that you probably misjudged your fitness. You shouldn't have assumed you could pedal down the road shooting the breeze with just anybody.

Maybe it's time you rethought your training program. Quality miles would help, maybe intervals. To be honest, you could lose a few pounds. Maybe cross-train, toughen up other muscle groups.

You could consider a new sport. Or no sport — that's it — you should forget about athletics. Yes. Face it. You aren't cut out for athletics, you should be home watching Hollywood Squares, you should be eating Egg McMuffins, you should quit, quit, quit.

You wonder what could have attracted you to cycling. You have no aptitude, no promise, no style. You gave it your shot. You bought good equipment. You tried. You even fooled yourself a while, thinking you liked it. What a laugh.

It dawns on you that the earlier wonderfulness of the day and the road and the bike and the conversation are burnt to white ash now. You are this minute considering suicide as an attractive alternative to this eternal, infernal chase.

You're roasting in half-wheel hell, 18 recurring inches from what promised to be a lovely, Sunday morning outing. Stripped of moral strength, stripped of every scrap of self-worth, you finish the ordeal. You say goodbye to your friend, "good ride, call you during the week."

The lie tastes copper in your mouth. You watch him pedal away, gone, around the corner. You're relieved now, but still a shattered, disillusioned wreck.

You focus what little emotional juice you have left onto hating him. You wish you held a little, stuffed, half-wheeler doll in your hands, in a little striped jersey just like his. You long for a sharpened stainless steel spoke. A mountain bike one.

I know how you feel; I've been half-wheeled myself.

When I am president of Pelotonia, half-wheeling will be as illegal as argyle cycling socks. The law books will say: "Half-wheeling; felonious training-ride mental abuse, usually a serial offense. First conviction punishable by shunning, heavy fines, confiscation of CX, CG tires. Second offense, two to four seasons at Pelotonian hard labor: assembly and adjustment of discount store bicycles to rigorous standards. No cable sports, no chocolate, no cycling magazines."

Ignorance of the law wouldn't cut it as an excuse either, dude, no way. Not in my courts.

I know they do it unconsciously. I don't care. Don't hand me that "They know not what they do," stuff. Won't sway me. What about us victims, the human emotional wreckage strewn in a half-wheeler's path?

I admit some may have otherwise admirable natures. One may have served honorably in the Peace Corps teaching framebuilding to hopelessly unemployed Taiwanese welders.

Another may have successfully protested noise violations at Vicenza during Campy's early indexed shifting tests. Yet another is rumored to have borrowed Laurent Fignon's helmet and tri-bars before that final Tour stage. No matter.

I've searched: I can find no forgiveness, though I seek down deep in my soul — down about 18 inches.

YOU BIKERS

About 20 of us passed a solo rider up a long, gentle grade. Going down the other side, he came by us on the yellow line, intent, obviously in a hurry. Just as he got around, we came to a red light. We stopped and so did he, but only momentarily. He looked both ways, took off through the red and was gone. We caught him at the next light.

I said, "Hey, how did you think that made us look, all 20 of us, when you ran that light in front of so many drivers?" He looked blankly at me and pulled away through the red. End of incident.

A week later, my friend Jennifer and I pedaled out through the same suburban area. A guy in a Rabbit pickup turned left across two lanes, close across in front of us, into a parking lot. I followed him in. "Did you see us?" I asked him through his window, "Did you see us?" He stared straight ahead. He'd thought that when he'd cut us off, that'd be it. But there I was. He opened his door, satisfied I wasn't going to assault him or kick his truck. He got out, a regular-looking guy, middle-fifties, carrying a folder of papers. A contractor, maybe, not a redneck. Somebody's dad.

"Sure I saw you," he said. "Why did you turn in front of us?" "Because I felt like it," he said. "Oh, then you have a license to do just about anything you feel like," I suggested. "Yeah," he said, "just like you bikers. You do any damn thing you feel like, running lights and taking advantage...."

"I see," I said, "you're a vigilante. You're gonna get revenge for all the things we cyclists do wrong." "No," he said, "I'm not a vigilante...."

"Then you're a cop. Are you a cop?" "No, I'm not a cop," he answered, and began to tell me about more evil things he'd seen bikers do.

"If you're not a vigilante and not a cop," I asked him, "what business is this of yours? Why would you endanger and scare two people you've never met? I don't understand." "That's it," he explained to me, "you simply don't understand." That's what he said: "simply." Then he turned his button-down-shirted back and walked away.

He was wrong, though: I *do* understand. I understand traffic is nightmarish in urban areas; drivers live with frustration and tension I'd find unbearable. Meanwhile, cycling's on the increase in busy areas, and cyclists take advantage where drivers can see. We do.

When we break laws where drivers — feeling impatient and impotent — can see us, we invite future confrontations. Mostly, the cyclist who eventually gets confronted will not be the one who started the driver's slow burn. Innocent or not, we lose.

I think some of us lose perspective of our role as road users. We imagine we're out there for reasons somehow more holy than drivers' reasons. We're not polluting the air. We're not clogging up the roads. We're not wasting resources. We're treading softly on the world. We shouldn't have to suffer under laws made for cars, we think.

We forget how visible we are to hundreds of drivers every day, while operating under a different system of laws — one we've conveniently adopted for ourselves.

I'm not saying vigilante drivers are right; of course they're not right. We don't harm *them*, but their perception of what we do can harm *us*. Precise legality doesn't matter; many drivers hate motorcyclists who split freeway lanes here in California, and lane-splitting is legal.

Those vigilantes can all go to hell — if it's up to me — but they won't. They'll still be there on the roads we ride. We're dealing ourselves a hand that has to lose. Look at us. We're outnumbered, outgunned and defended by one or two layers of Lycra-spandex.

You gamble big-time when you flagrantly abuse your rights on the road. You gamble when you run a light while people in cars look on. You gamble when you ride out in traffic, in front of a lengthening parade of cars, inside some of which — no doubt — lurk resentful hotheads.

You're betting your own (and my) already frail good standing in those drivers' eyes. You stand to lose big by creating, one violated stoplight at a time, a latently lethal, spiteful driving public. You're betting a lot, dude. You're betting our lives.

911

■ 'd ridden down that trail before, but as soon as we turned off the road and began the rutted, dust-slippery, steep, single-track descent, I felt "off," intimidated. I imagined myself crashing.

I ride descents like that one with my rear brake locked and tire skidding. I crab down, using the front brake only when I think I can get away with it. Maybe Ned Overend rides them at 30 mph, but I don't — I skid the tire and crab.

Because I felt unusually slow and uncertain, I pulled over to the side of the trail and let my buddies, Dave and Robert, go by. No sense getting in the way. I looked back up the hill; no sign of our fourth rider, Derek. I started down the hill. I remember that as I began rolling I felt clumsy — I had trouble getting my second foot in its clip. I remember the bike was pointed at a good-sized rut.

That's *all* I remember — I woke up lying in the trail. Several paramedics hovered over me, asking me questions: "What day is today?" "Where are we?" I felt pretty "with-it" and thought my answers sounded okay, *cool* even. I remember telling the guy examining me that, if he touched me *there*, he'd better mean it.

Derek, I learned, had seen the dust-cloud my crash generated; saw a prone figure and thought it was Robert, who'd begun the descent immediately in front of him. When he checked, though, sure enough; it was me — unconscious, mouth open, rattling noises coming out, tongue flapping, one ear all bloody. Gross.

Freaked ol' Derek out. He ran up the trail to a house and called 911. About then, Robert and David, up ahead somewhere, concluded that half the group had failed to follow them down the hill. Stopping to wait, they heard sirens and, shaking their heads, started walking their bikes back up the hill. When they reached me, the paramedics were already on the scene.

First, I got carried up the steep hill on a high-tech board by three guys who had to set me down a couple of times on the way. Then I got the lights-and-sirens ambulance ride. I stared up at the diamond-plate ceiling while the guys stuck I-Vs in my arms and asked me questions. It felt, of course, as if it were happening to someone else.

Somehow, somebody removed my beloved, battered, orange rain jacket, given to me by my friend Penny, several years ago; and my jersey, a beautiful, multi-colored Casati (bicycles) one given to me last spring by Signore Casati in Monza. At the hospital, however, trauma-team personnel cut my polypro tee-shirt, shorts and tights off me. Sliced my favorite, ancient, holey-butt, double-front bib tights.... damn.

Ten hours at the hospital, holding Shelly's hand. Chest X-rays. One or two broken ribs. Concussion. Double vision. CT scan. Scrapes and bruises here and there, a helmet-strap burn in front of my left ear, cuts above my left eye and on my right ear. The blood that worried Derek did not come from inside my head, but simply from the cuts. Simply.

My Bell helmet (thank goodness for that helmet, given to me a year or so ago by my buddy, Don Davis, of Bell) took most of the impact on the left temple area. Today, the micro-shell remains intact. The ground chewed up the polystyrene liner where it's exposed below the shell. When you look inside, you see cracked lining and glued-in sizing pads that have been forcibly moved around. You can see blood stains on the lining and the shell.

As I type this, eight days after the crash, my broken-rib side hurts like mad. I have to close one eye so I can make out the words on my computer screen. I'm hoping the double vision will go away, that one morning I'll wake up and mysteriously it'll be gone. Meanwhile, I can't drive or ride — I can't decide which center line is the real one.

I've thought about trail riding quite a bit. It seems to me that I won't do it again without at least one companion. Had no one been with me when I crashed, who *knows* how long I'd have been there, how long it would've taken me to find help. Luckily, we were on the edge of civilization, very near a phone.

You could say that I might've been going slower if I'd have been alone, that there would've been less pressure to keep up with the guys. Maybe. I bet I wasn't traveling five mph when I crashed.

I don't think I'll do much riding without a helmet, either. I bet I can get Don Davis to send me another Bell. And I believe I'll pay more attention when that voice tells me I'm not quite focussed on riding my bike, too.

You know, I hadn't crashed for several years. Maybe I won't crash again for an equally long time, maybe longer. Still, I think I've spent as much time in the trauma center as I'd like. Not that the folks at Highland Hospital weren't nice; I don't want to sound ungrateful.

I'm going to try to ride carefully. I'll try to remember, even after I've been riding crash-free for months or years, that eventually I'll crash again. Probably *will* crash again, huh?

How about you? Why don't you, too, try to ride carefully. We'll ride carefully together, you and me, but separately, because you're there and I'm here. Let's do it. Whattaya say?

A DOZEN HAIRPINS

June 5, 5:30 a.m.; Ortesei, Italy, in the Dolomite Mountains....
Couldn't sleep. I'm typing at a table in the deserted bar downstairs in our hotel, waiting for someone to show up to fix my first cappuccino. I've only been in Italy for a day and already my head is spinning.

Yesterday. Yesterday had to be one of the best days I've ever experienced, on and off the bike. Three mountain passes ridden back-and-forth; 10-mile climbs and descents; absolutely world-class scenery; a great hotel, and the nicest people to ride with and hang around with afterwards.

I'm here courtesy of the association of Italian bike and bike parts manufacturers and Breaking Away Bicycle Tours. The Breaking Away people take care of my lodging and van transportation. The bike association made sure I had a first-class Italian racing bicycle on which to explore these unbelievable roads.

My bike's a Basso: A round steel-tube, straight-ahead racing bike painted red-and-silver fade. It never put a wheel wrong in the 60-odd miles I rode yesterday on unfamiliar and (shall we say) challenging roads.

Right away it felt like *my* bike, exactly the way a good bicycle should — especially when the sky threatens rain and the rider is far from home, somewhat fried from jet-lag and prone to grumpiness.

This Basso is full Campagnolo ErgoPower-equipped, Chorus parts. The stuff works great. Never having ridden a brake lever-shifting setup, I wasn't sure what to expect. I needn't have worried; the new shifting works exactly the way it's supposed to. I will resist going back to frame-mounted levers. These are just too easy to use, always there, right near your fingers. You do shift more, just as people say.

I'm especially grateful they shift so well because I've used every gear on the bike, I promise. I think I have 39x24. One more tooth on the front or one fewer on the back and I'd have been in trouble. Can't be out of the saddle all the way up a 10-mile climb; you have to be able to sit down and turn the gear.

Here's how the day went. The previous night at dinner, Breaking Away tour leaders gave us maps, highlighted in three colors, and advice to help each of us choose his or her next day's ride route. You could choose from routes of two or three distances and levels of difficulty.

Then, breakfast in the hotel at 7 a.m: rolls, three kinds of preserves, muesli, yogurt with strawberries, on and on. A pot of "American coffee" and a pitcher of steamed milk. Give me eight, maybe 10 years; I could get bored with breakfasts like these.

Then, yesterday, a ride in a Breaking Away van to Corvara, where the Giro d'Italia stage would finish about four o' clock in the afternoon. The bikes come off the van roofs. Front wheels go on, and off we go on whatever adventure we chose. Riding alone, with a group, fast, slow, however we want.

Later we will meet back here and put on warmups. We'll watch, with thousands of lunatic Italian fans, the finish of the 13th stage of the 75th Tour of Italy. Half-an-hour after the finish, we hop back in the vans and head for the next hotel, a shower and one more dynamite dinner.

Does that sound good? It does? It was.

Breaking Away has its act polished. Some of the riders on this trip have already done three or four Breaking Away tours, here at the Giro or at the Tour de France. The staff's knowledge of the roads and countryside is amazing. They take care of everything. Let's say it rains during the day. When you go to get your bike the next morning, the Breaking Away mechanic has wiped it down and re-oiled the chain.

Oops. I have to take a break now and reload my word processor: I'm running out of superlative adjectives.

I love being here in Italy, especially in the mountains, in the small towns. It's great watching people here, the way they talk to each other, the relaxed way they kid around. Seems to me there's something about living that we Americans have forgotten or never knew, but that is second nature to these Italians.

The riding here is so superior you wonder how you can face putting in the miles back home. You pass the ruins of a castle at the top of a hill. You drop down to the valley floor through about a dozen hairpins, real hairpins; you find you're grinning and can't quit.

The legions of fans on the roadsides cheered us as we climbed the long hills on the race route. A couple of us who looked especially tired on the climbs got pushed by fans. A 20-yard heave at the right moment can help, I've been told.

Today, we're supposed to climb a more difficult pass, steeper, we hear, than anything we encountered yesterday. But hey — I'm not nervous. My red-and-silver

Basso and I will roll right over anything these Dolomites and Giro routes can put in our path. No worries.

A bicycle seems at home here, appropriate, not only to you but to the drivers and pedestrians. Maybe, maybe, there's a better place to ride a bike than here in the north of Italy.

I doubt it.

104 DEGREES

Near Wichita Falls, Texas … August … 80 miles into the Hotter 'N Hell Hundred. Sure it's hot. What'd you expect from north Texas in summer, up here near the Oklahoma line? Why else would they call this the Hotter'N Hell?

Heat's a headliner here; wind's the backup band. Texoma winds don't gust and knock you around. Oh no. Texoma headwinds lean into you, push on your chest, hold your cyclometer numbers down in the low teens.

A hundred miles in 104-degree Wichita Falls heat takes a long time at 13 point 5 mph. Long time.

Texoma terrain's not so bad; wind and heat're enough. After 50 or 60 miles you thought was easy rolling, that small chainring starts looking mighty good.

Something out here in the Texas countryside saps you. Says to you: Hey, that last little hill felt harder than it should've. Better pull into the next rest stop, get something cold to drink, maybe pour over your head.

A rest stop can't be much farther; HTH sets them up every 10 miles, and it's a good thing they do. Heat problems slip up on you. You start to feel lightheaded, a little wobbly on your bike. Like now.

Oh good. There's a series of little verse signs leading to the rest stop: "You've tried the rest, now stop at the best," like old Burma Shave ads. Volunteers dressed as Superman and Mighty Mouse are out in the road directing traffic. Even lightheaded and wobbly, you can get in and out without problems.

You coast over to one of the poles supporting the huge canvas canopy, intending to lean your bike on the pole. Before you get your second foot unclipped, an HTH volunteer runs over with a tray of large glasses of Sparkletts ice water, straight or with Exceed.

You down a frosty paper cup of Exceed in seconds. A wave of "okay" rushes over you. You lean your precious bike against something, anything, glad to have it out of your sight. You step under the canopy, out of the relentless Texoma sun.

You stall there, trying to decide whether to stand still in the shade, sit on a lawn chair or chaise lounge, or go for some fruit or cookies. A nurse, smiling, wearing a stethoscope, walks up. How're you doing, she asks. She looks at your eyes, listens to your answers. Confident you're okay, she smiles, walks away looking for another refugee from the heat.

A smiling guy with a military-short haircut reaches into a 55-gallon drum of ice cubes, pulls out a rented white towel, hands it to you. You wipe salt off your face and out of your hair. You chill the back of your neck with the wonderful icy white towel. What an invention, the towel, you think.

After a minute, the guy takes back your wonderful towel, hands you a freshie. An even better towel. You love the guy and grin at him. He grins back. Where do they find these people, you wonder. Like this towel guy. And the nurse. So nice.

Later, you'll read that there are 3000 Wichita Falls people, 700 of 'em medical workers, helping 13,000 cyclists on this ride. All those volunteers smiling, friendly, genuinely concerned with how you're doing. Amazing, Texas. Amazing.

A moment of weakness hits you, unused as you are to the heat, spoiled by cool Northern California. You decide to opt for the chaise lounge, and right now would be fine, thank you. You half sit, half fall, down onto the chair.

The nurse and the towel guy hover over you. A third support worker, a woman, shows up with slices of melon. A fourth offers a tray of iced drinks.

Someone hands you a glass of Exceed. The towel guy puts fresh white terry cloth, ice cubes rolled in it, on your forehead. The nurse looks at your eyes and skin for signs of what happens to riders who do too much in this much heat. She smiles; you must look okay.

The towel guy suddenly, in quick swipes, drapes three iced towels across your dusty, sweaty, aching legs. A cold delicious rush breaks over you, indescribable in a family cycling publication.

The iced-towels-across-the-legs thrill causes you to moan in a way you seldom do in public places. The towel guy grins. You think: I love the towel guy. I'll never forget you, you tell him. And you don't.

The nurse grins too, says, "Better than sex, isn't it?"

Oh yes, you answer. And lasts so much longer, too.

I'M A ROAD-RUNNER HON-EE

Two-part story. In the first part, I'm riding by myself, climbing up Wildcat Canyon Road, above Berkeley. I'm sitting in the saddle, easily turning the 19 (okay, the 21) and sweating behind my sunglasses. My eyes are starting to sting.

I see a guy on a bike; black shorts; cables showing; nice, old Univega; stopped on the shoulder, facing against traffic. I slow, but not much—can't slow much from my uphill speed, not without toppling over.

I say, "Hi, how you doin'?"

The guy looks at me, points into the grassy field rolling away from the road and says, "There's a coyote."

I steer onto the shoulder. Just like he said, maybe 40 feet away, other side of a wire fence, I see a pointy-nosed, bushy-tailed, medium-size-dog-sized coyote. Wow.

Note: We see deer here in the San Francisco Bay urban-suburban sprawl. We see an occasional rabbit, skunk, possum or raccoon, but we do not often see a coyote. I'd never seen one.

For a minute or two the guy and I stand on the shoulder by our bikes watching the coyote, hardly speaking. The coyote seems not to be bothered by us. Calmly, he surveys the grassy hillside, glancing over once or twice in case one of us has a rifle. Why should he trust us? He may not know any bike riders.

We begin to talk. We speak of how uncommon it is to see such an animal, and how remarkably un-mangy this one looks. We agree it appears lean and capable, not flea-bitten, scarred, or raggedy-eared. A fine, prosperous coyote; takes care of itself. Not Wiley Coyote, Rotary Coyote.

After a while, bored with the view or with our conversation, the coyote wanders over the brow of the hill. We can just see the tips of his pointy ears in the long grass. We watch his ears for a couple minutes — shows how often we see coyotes

— then we climb back on the bikes, sorry it's over.

Turns out we're both headed up the hill and back down into Berkeley. My new friend's a grad student at Cal, in environmental studies, so we do not lack for conversational fodder. Lots of environment out there (why, it's all around us) and plenty of problems to complain about. We have a great chat.

You can probably imagine our conversation. As one car after another whizzes by us so charmingly, we discuss our natural enemy as cyclists, the *car*. We're neither of us *car* guys.

We complain about how many *cars* we see, and how few people we see in each *car*. We mutter about visible air. We bitch about how inappropriate, how wasteful *cars* are. We marvel at the amazing emotional changes wrought in otherwise gentle people while they are inside *cars*.

We agree we cannot, as a nation, afford the horrible price we pay for our addiction to casual use of six-passenger *cars* as solo daily runabouts. And we talk about the impossibility of our doing anything about any of the above, except by example. We can "shut up and ride our bikes."

Before we get to the top of the hill, we're friends. We have mutual adversaries. We trust each other. He says his name is Jeff; I say mine's Maynard. We say we hope we run into each other again. He turns left up Grizzly Peak; I go straight.

I feel great. I saw a coyote and had a satisfying, 30-minute bonding experience; things like that should happen to me every day. That's the first part of the story.

In the second part I'm having lunch with my friend Rom, who's way smarter than me. We've ordered breakfast in the early afternoon, and while we wait for our food, I'm telling him about the coyote ride.

I tell Rom about pedaling up Wildcat, seeing the guy on the hill, about the guy pointing, about the two of us watching the coyote. I tell him about the conversation the guy and I had, the almost instant friendship.

I tell him about how seeing the coyote and chatting with the nice guy transformed what was an otherwise ordinary bike ride and turned it into an afternoon in a hundred.

Rom looks at me, considers, says he knows exactly why I saw the coyote. I hesitate, trying to figure what he means. I wonder what karmic or mystical explanation he's got in mind for me. It was just luck I saw the coyote, I decide. What does he mean? I draw a blank.

"Okay," I say finally, "why'd I see the coyote?"

"Because you stopped," Rom says, "and asked the guy how he was doing."

I told you he was smarter than me.

IT'S THE LAW

You can divide bike riders into two groups: those who believe in their hearts that cycling is an aerodynamic sport — and those who would rather deny it. Those who draft, those who don't.

Cycling is certainly all about the movement of air, particularly when there's more than one cyclist around. Group riding techniques are based on aerodynamic truths and how cyclists can use them.

A rider who is unpracticed in group skills is merely an athlete on a bike, half-educated, a pedaler. To my mind, he or she is not a complete cyclist; no matter how strong; no matter if that person is a triathlete, a 30-century-a-year veteran or a RAAM winner.

Road cycling's aerodynamic truths care nothing about gender, age or politics — they're physical science. Denying those truths is like denying gravity: You won't change gravity. As they say, it's the law.

Miguel Indurain couldn't win one road race without drafting. Tactical cycling, all road cycling above the fundamental level, is drafting. You can only feel so proud of your cycling, I'd say, if you don't know how — or are covertly unwilling — to draft.

No doubt some people will be stronger than others on any ride. Nevertheless, with proper group technique, the draft will allow the following rider to sit in at 80 percent effort. Even on long, fast rides, everyone above a certain level of fitness can keep up. Everyone can have fun.

Riders who deny the need to practice group skills will make that same long day into a ride-and-wait death march, a strain on themselves and their partners.

Proficient road riders make the most of the strength of others, especially when they feel least fit. Using others' strength costs nothing but the commitment to stay on a wheel, in the draft. Why is that commitment so difficult for some otherwise accomplished cyclists to make?

Savvy road cyclists learned drafting from racing-experienced friends who would not take no for an answer. Sit on, someone told the newcomer, don't come off the wheel. If he or she did come off, the group waited once or twice then went on ahead. Eventually, the new rider learned to stay on a wheel.

If your sport-cycling friends wait for you, indulge you, never expect you to take the least advantage of the draft offered by stronger riders, that's your loss. Why learn anything new? Why sit in? They'll wait.

You may resist drafting because you already feel defeated. Hell, you can't do it, you'll just get dropped and feel worse. Better not try. All cyclists, you may think, who ride in pace-lines and groups and wear team jerseys are stronger, faster than you are. You wouldn't stand a chance.

After all, they're serious riders — and you, why, you ride no more than five times a week and no more than three centuries a month. You probably spend no more than 30 percent of your disposable income on bike stuff, read every bike mag and buy all the books....

And yet you won't even draft behind people you know you can trust beyond question. Can't be fear of crashing keeping you from doing it. Curious, isn't it?

Let's say you can maintain 17 mph by yourself on a certain stretch of road or in a flat century. You won't draft. Your riding buddies could, for the sake of argument, average two mph more over the same route. If you don't sit in, don't rest on a wheel and use the draft to enhance your strength, the fastest your group can proceed is your comfortable solo speed. No more. You control the ride from the back.

If that's OK, if that's what you feel you have to do to enjoy your cycling among friends, keep doing just that.

No one said you *have* to draft. Thousands of riders have pedaled millions of miles disdaining the draft, staring into the somber face of physics and insisting, nonetheless, that its principles don't apply — not to them. "I can't do it. I'll get dropped."

Experienced riders look at the wheel in front of them as a lifeline, as their connection to the group, to cycling beyond pedaling. They think of group riding as a precise discipline that makes them faster, that helps them improve, that provides a fun social and fitness experience — not a long, lonely slog out and back.

Inexperienced or unwilling riders hang back five feet — might as well be five miles. Pace picks up half a mile per hour and they're dropped. They know it'll happen; always has. They do it anyway.

A group passes them on the road, going one mph faster. They keep up easily with the group, five feet back. Group picks up its pace one mph: dropped.

They never do the tiny bit of work it takes to get on that wheel, to grab that opportunity because — I'm increasingly convinced — they've made up their minds they're not good enough. Not even good enough to try.

No hill so steep, no wind so cruel, as a mind set against itself.

EXORCISING DEMONS

'm not feeling too good right now. I just heard that five cyclists out training on the Central Coast of California got nailed by a car. A driver swerved across two-and-a-half lanes and hit them, killing one guy and badly hurting another. The driver was drunk....

And not just *kinda* drunk. He'd raised his blood alcohol level to .025 by 10 o'clock on a weekday morning: He had two-and-a-half times the legal limit of booze in his bloodstream.

Thinking about drunk driving always makes me a little crazy.

I know we take chances out on the road. Obnoxious motorists and close-calls come with the territory. I figure if I want to ride the road, I have to deal with its hazards. A drunk, though, is another thing — the wild card in the pedaling (or motoring) deck.

You can do everything right: stop at stop signs, signal your turns, wear a helmet (hell, wear *two* helmets), bright colors and reflective clothing. Wear a suit of armor, anything. None of it'll help if some half-loaded dude in his Firebird drops a lighted Marlboro in his lap at 60 mph. By the time he's sure he won't burn his whatchacal-lit, you and he may have tried to occupy the same space on the road. A hassle for him, a hospital visit for you — with luck.

And we protect that drunk driver in this country. A drunk driver's thought of as a solid citizen who's made a judgment mistake; a good man or woman, probably, caught in awful circumstances. Jail? No, not for a single, momentary lapse. Even if the consequences were tragic.

But, hey, you've heard that stuff before. And what can you do, really? I've got no glib answer, but I *do* know one thing we can do. Most likely it won't make a bit of difference, but it feels right: We can be examples.

We can not drink. We can absolutely not drink if we're going anywhere near our bikes or a motor vehicle. We can realize that if we believe a *little* alcohol is okay — but more is too much — we're fooling ourselves the same way drunk drivers do.

A little alcohol is just *less* poison than more alcohol.

We can gently make our anti-drinking feelings known to friends. We can make it convenient not to drive for persons we know to be drinking.

Sounds hard-line, doesn't it? Maybe drinking's okay. Some people appear to carry it off quite well. The spirits industry surrounds us with images of men and women enjoying alcohol in moderation, men and women we'd like to know, look and act like.

People in the booze ads (and the cigarette ads) apparently live terrific, fulfilling lives, unlike our boring, not-nearly-perfect lives. They refresh themselves spiritually and physically with alcohol.

We don't meet those people, though, do we, in our world? We never get to walk with them through balmy, early-summer fields, wearing loose clothing and satisfied (but never smug) smiles, carrying wicker baskets of bottles and brie, and smoking because we enjoy it.

We meet the people who enjoy alcohol out on the grimy edge of the highway. We appear in our salty Lycra; they're driving home after enjoying fine, refreshing spirits in the company of friends.

Sometimes, after such adult, sophisticated libation, they make navigational errors and rudely drive into us, surprising us. A tragic mistake, but not life-changing — not for them. Somebody down at the bar will know a good lawyer.

It occurs to me that certain terrific cycling events are brought to us by the gentle folks who make the spirit beverages I'm begging you not to drink. I love those events; I'd hate to lose even one of them.

But even if every one of you reading this quits drinking today, and quietly advocates temperance forever, the sales curves of brewers and distillers will not droop. We'd quit because we thought it was right, not because it would work.

When you put down this book and look around, you'll see billboard, magazine and TV ads featuring worthy individuals enjoying adult beverages in festive, supportive surroundings. The booze industry can afford to place opinion-shaping ads anywhere they like.

But I can't. And *I'm* trying to shape your opinion, too. I'd like you to look at those ads (and the drinking they promote) in a new way. This column is my own black-and-white ad for non-consumption: a note in a bottle floating in a sea of "drinking-is-hip" propaganda.

Think of it as a reminder. Booze ads are expensively produced, clever and effective; it's easy to forget that they lie. Why, even the 'party animal" is a fake — a fictional device, created for effect. And Spuds is a dog someone clever invented — like Cujo....

MAYNARD'S NO-CHARGE ROAD RIDING GUIDE

More people than ever ride bicycles these days. Sadly, much of the advice available to riders is misinformation, lies, brainless superstition and worse. I have taken it upon myself to clear the air, and not a moment too soon, I might add.

Many so-called rules about road cycling are not rules at all. They're merely conclusions riders have reached after years of experience. Maybe those conclusions are correct; maybe not. Let's examine a few.

First, or No.1: "You can't trust car drivers." Surely you've heard that one. It's simply wrong. Car drivers are the most dependable creatures you will encounter out there on the road. Compared with unpredictables such as some farmer's dog, laughably misnamed "man's best friend," drivers are dead dependable.

You can depend on drivers to do the convenient thing. That truth made 7-Eleven enough money to support an international bicycle racing team, even without employing English-speaking counter help.

Let me illustrate. Let's say a driver sees no other vehicles or pedestrians around, just you, on your bicycle. If that driver senses that no witness can cause him embarrassment or legal inconvenience, and if he feels that it might be fun to move you over a little with his car, most likely he will. You can depend on it.

And can you blame him, really? It's his (or her) road, after all, and there you are, out in it again. If he's unusually courteous, he may merely throw some object at you from his car. If that object turns out to be light in weight, free of sharp edges and/or empty of disgusting mystery liquids, thank your lucky stars and your state's driver-awareness program.

But remember — you can't always expect to be that lucky. You foolishly believed stupid notion #2: "Bicyclists have a right to part of the (paved) roadway." New riders are provided with that ticking bomb of misinformation every day. That's like telling folks to treat firearms as if they're squirt guns. Hey, it's criminal.

Rule #3: "Flat tires come in threes." You will hear bikies nationwide recite that nonsense as if it were gospel. Listen to me: You don't have to get flat tires at all. None. It's a trick. Here's how.

First, install new, high-quality tires and tubes. Use new, cotton rim tapes. Liberally talc the tapes, the tubes and the insides of the tires. Inflate carefully to recommended pressure; check your manual if necessary. Do not, I repeat, do not over-inflate. You can under-inflate up to 10 percent if you weigh less than 145 pounds.

Then, park your bike, leaning the handlebars and seat against a wall in your living room after vacuuming the area carefully. Close the drapes or choose a wall that's never exposed to direct sunlight. Wait seven days, check your tire pressures, add air as necessary. Repeat at least once a week.

Between pressure checks, do not remove your bike from the room. You'll find you've totally eliminated the flat tire nuisance: You may simply give up carrying a spare. Plus (this should surprise and please you) you will find the glossy, grey-anodized sides of those high-budget rims remain unscratched and pristine, almost indefinitely. It's like a bonus.

Now tell me. Aren't you glad you read this story? Don't you love this book, where you can get really helpful advice like that, without writing some "expert" a stupid-sounding letter?

The "sounding stupid" idea brings us to silly idea #4: "Ride a straight line." What a bore. Hey, *anyone* can ride a straight line. It takes class and confidence to cast tradition aside, to decide that those other guys can learn to ride the way *you* do, the crooked way. Your way.

Do you think people said to Fausto Coppi: Fausto, ride a straight line? Hell, no. If they could keep up and still breathe enough to speak, they said, Fausto, ride any way you want. Do you think a man like, say, Peewee Herman, got famous riding *straight?*

And the last of this advice, dogmatic maxim #5: "Ride in low gears." What a tyranny. Hey I'm serious; what are we running here, a free country, or what? Why'd we fight all those wars, in Europe and France and Cuba?

You wanna ride in low gears, more power to you. But if you wanna ride in jams and a Bon Jovi tanktop, get it on, homie. If you wanna ride in New England in the autumn for the turning leaves, enjoy. If you wanna train in pain, in a caffeine-fueled drive for fitness nirvana, go for it, 110 percent, minimum. Fax me your personal best.

You wanna ride in LeMondster gears, smash and pound, rock and roll on mondo-ratios? Just Do It. You wanna flatten hills in the big ring? You wanna snap crankarms off at the spindle? You wanna see if the frame stiffness you paid for when you laid that gold card on the counter is all there, like the man said it would be? Just ... do ... it.

You only go around once.

Still, you might want to pull on some leg-warmers on nippy fall days. You may want to rub something hot on your knees and warm up a couple of low-gear miles on chilly Sunday mornings. Couldn't hurt. Just in case there might be something to those cobwebbed old bikie clichés after all.

While you're out there, those crisp Sunday mornings, you might see a guy pedaling real slow, struggling a little, possibly. The guy might be wearing what looks like snazzy, new, Italian bike clothing. Be sure and wave. Might be me. After all the tips I've given you this month, no charge, I know you wouldn't want to hurt my feelings.

IT'S TUESDAY, THIS MUST BE BERGAMO

'll bet you spent your early-April days on the wind trainer, listening to old Fleetwood Mac tapes. I can see you there, acid sweat dripping on your top tube, bored to the bone, staring slack-jawed out a steamy window at endlessly dreary weather.

Me? Oh, I went to Italy with my wife and my bike. Shelly and I stayed two weeks at a posh hotel in Milan. She worked, I rode, we ate wonderful dinners together. It was pretty neat.

You'll be pleased to hear it was so warm there that I wore shorts and short sleeves on the road. I had to put sunblock on my ears or they'd have burned. Might've been uncomfortable. Sorry for me? Oh.

Each day I'd head north, through Monza, then pick a destination. One Sunday I rode to Madonna del Ghissalo, the Coppi shrine. Twice I rode to Montevecchia, the highest point in Brianza, and once to Lake Como.

I also pedaled over to Bergamo, where the Settimana Bergamasca (pro-am) stage race was starting. I stayed three days with national coach Chris Carmichael and the U.S. Team, including eventual overall winner Lance Armstrong. I ate with the guys and rode with Chris in the team car during a stage.

The following day, I drove a feed van for Eddie B, who was short a soigneur, and handed bottles (badly — you'd have done it better) to his Subaru-Montgomery guys.

Eddie loaned me a great-looking Subaru-Montgomery jersey to wear so the guys could see me in the busy feed zone; afterwards he let me keep it. Looks nearly as good on me as it would on you.

Now, about the riding: In Milan, the aggressive traffic; the (expletive deleted) streetcar tracks; the occasional stretches of flat, but unevenly laid paving stones;

the slow bikes and mopeds in the curb "lane"; and the almost indecipherable (to me) signal lights made urban pedaling somewhat demanding. The locals do fine, naturally, but I was generally nervous. There you are in urban Italy, surrounded by wonderful things to see, but you don't dare look.

On your bike, you don't command a lane or a few feet of roadway as we do here in the U.S. You command about 20 inches. Your pedal brushes the curb on the right; traffic polishes your elbow on the left.

Outside of town, on wider two-lane roads, you get the same 20 inches. Drivers never hesitate; they put the right front fender 20 1/2 inches from the edge of the road, and come around. If you see something in your path that you would steer around at home, you ride right over it. No fastidious swerving here in Italy. You get so you can ride a damn straight line.

Driving on the road in Italy reminded me of race-caravan driving in America. No other traffic situation in the U.S. seems even remotely similar. It works because of the amazing skill of Italian drivers.

Drop one Connecticut commuter in his Cherokee into this choreography, and you'd need a thousand tow trucks and the national guard to clear away the carnage. Might be weeks before they'd get an accurate bike-rider body count. Have to count bottom-bracket axles — and *they'd* be bent.

You soon get over your homegrown distrust of the drivers. You realize that if you just ride predictably, in a straight line, no one will hit you. That's an observation, not a promise.

Out in the country you can ride further out in the road if you must, or two cyclists can ride side-by-side; cars will still pass you without hesitation. But they will merely pass — no honking, no fist-shaking, no agony.

Italian drivers are aggressive, no doubt, but they are typically not *hostile*. There's a perceptible difference. They drive fast and take advantage of holes in traffic — like a racer jockeying in a criterium — but they mind their own business.

They do not assume they know what's best for other people. They don't cruise in the left lane on the motorway, controlling the speed of everyone behind them. They don't honk at bicyclists or moped riders who ignore traffic signals or pass between cars when traffic is stopped.

Speaking of driving…. A six-man team from China came to the Settimana Bergamasca with eight support people. The support crew went to the race office to pick up their team car. When they were handed the keys, they asked the race people who would drive the car. "Why, one of *you* will," was the reply.

"Oh, but none of *us* can drive," said the eight Chinese.

Virtually all the cyclists I saw were men (maybe I remember *one* woman), and mostly over 40. You see young guys out training, club racers or an occasional pro, and you see old guys.

Most of them look good on their bikes, better than the general run of U.S. cyclists, but they do not go especially fast. At the pace I ride — pitifully slow, based on my hometown club ride standards — I blew by almost everyone. They ride straight and smooth, cooperate well in groups and look great — they simply aren't going really fast.

I believe cycling is more mature there; a regular, comfortable part of life for people, not a kicky new enthusiasm. They're practicing a healthy discipline, not getting ready for something (training, training) the way so many of us imagine *we* are. Fewer dangling carrots in Italy.

SO THAT'S WHAT IT'S LIKE

I'm a Caucasian male, third-generation American. It's dawning on me at gut level that we white guys get respect we don't have to earn. I didn't realize how completely I took that birthright for granted until I had a couple unpleasant, but instructive experiences.

First, I acquired a motorcycle that wasn't accepted by guys in the business. When it developed problems, I found that not only wasn't *it* taken seriously, as its owner, *I* was no longer taken seriously. I got no respect.

Mechanics would tap a foot while I explained a problem, only pretending to listen. Then they'd continue as if I hadn't described the problem or wouldn't know one if it came up and bit me. I'd never been treated that way before; it got old instantly.

I complained about it at a staff meeting of the motorcycle paper I write for. A woman writer said, "That's how women get treated all the time. Mechanics never take us seriously at all."

"Ah," I thought, "so *that's* what it's like."

Yesterday morning, I pedaled to work on busy suburban streets, meticulously staying out of the way of cars. As I rode a bare door-width from a line of parked cars, an American sedan skimmed by. The driver yelled at me, "So you like to play chicken with cars, asshole!"

I kept pedaling. A block up the street, the guy got stuck behind some cars waiting for a left-turner. I rode by on his right. He came up on my left, yelling furiously, and turned abruptly into the curb across my path — the way cops stop people on TV. I had to brake hard to keep from hitting his right rear fender.

I rode around the back of the car and continued up the street, hoping he'd lose interest. Nope. He came around and blocked me worse. I had to stop hard as I could to avoid crashing into him. I stayed there behind his car, astride my bike, waiting to see what he'd do next.

He jumped out, already screaming, and ran back at me. We did the over-the-handlebars face-off. He looked to be in his early or mid-30s, regular ol' working class guy. No baseball hat. Shorts and a tee-shirt. Probably takes some kid to the ballgame.

He said he thought I was out there primarily — maybe entirely — to harass drivers. It never occurred to him, I guess, that I might be going somewhere, not simply trying to ruin his life.

"You're wearing that hard-hat," he yelled, "so you can play around with cars and not get killed. You do the same stupid, pain-in-the-ass thing every day."

I could see he was sure he was right; communication was not in the cards. I suggested he get back in his car and get on with his day. Eventually, after repeatedly calling my ancestry and intelligence into question, he did. I finished my commute. When I stopped trembling, I thought about what'd happened.

A night or so earlier, my wife and I had seen the movie "Falling Down," with Michael Douglas. You've probably seen it. Douglas plays D-Fens: a wacko, recently fired defense worker who abandons his car and walks to his ex-wife's home against her wishes. She's so scared of him she's secured a court order banning him from the premises.

D-Fens thinks of himself as a model citizen, a hard-working, white "real American" whose job, family and way of life have been stolen by forces he can't control. None of it has been his fault.

He walks into a convenience store in a crummy neighborhood for phone change. The Korean-American owner, a Mr. Lee, if I remember correctly, resists providing phone change for non-customers. He charges high-ish prices the way convenience stores do. He's a first-generation immigrant and speaks accented English.

Lee is not evil. No way. He's merely trying to get along as best he can in a foreign, hostile, scary environment. Lee is you and I on our bicycles, on streets owned by cars.

D-Fens decides Lee's not there to run a business. He lives to make the lives of genuine Americans — hard-working, Caucasian Americans — miserable. Lee, visibly "different," is someone D-Fens can identify and blame for the loss of what he remembers as quality in his life.

D-Fens accuses Lee of refusing to pronounce English words right, refusing to lower his prices for a deserving, tax-paying, white guy, and refusing to be browbeaten by D-Fens' "We-white-Americans-carried-the-free-world" rhetoric.

D-Fens gets more upset by the moment. Lee becomes afraid. The two scuffle, and D-Fens grabs a baseball bat Lee keeps for protection. D-Fens wrecks the store, then, before leaving, makes a point of paying for a Coke at a special, low, white-guy price.

Like my car driver, D-Fens acted in offended rage, feeling absolutely, inarguably, right. "How'd I get to be the bad guy?" he asks. D-Fens remembers when Americans didn't have to put up with that crap. We had good jobs, drove new Chevys. Cokes were a quarter. Streets were clear of minorities and goddamn bicycles.

It's easy for us white guys to fall into feeling like D-Fens. We've had things our way for so long. Occasionally, we need to walk in the other guy's or gal's shoes.

When we're on our bikes, we're in those shoes. Some people, who think like D-Fens, believe cyclists exist solely to harass hard-working, "real" American motorists. Bike riders irritate them and look different; we're second-class citzens on the road, a minority easily identified as the problem.

Out there, we're the bad guys — like Korean storekeepers — just trying to do the best we can. Unless I miss my guess, that's what it's like.

FREE AT LAST

I gave myself a new mountain bike for Christmas. It's my second flirtation with off-road riding but this time it feels like it'll last. Several of my roadie friends recently bought mountain bikes, so the faces in our twice-a-week group haven't changed — only the riding surfaces.

Oh, we're all converted now; we're fat-tire enthusiasts. Ask us something, we'll go on and on. And we *should* go on and on: trail-riding's fun. Descending, I can scare myself most delightfully, all white knuckles and big, frozen grin, without exceeding 20 mph. Even long climbs are kinda fun. And kinda hard — I never have to hop off and push my road bike.

I miss the road? Not those couple of rides a week. I sure *don't* miss "sharing" the road with intercooled, mall-to-mall missiles piloted by caffeine-overdosed, joy-less, suburban moms 'n dads. I like the car-free hush out there in the hills.

I also like the subliminal mountain-bike workout. It sneaks up on you. People say life's what happens to you while you're planning your future; fitness happens the same way, by osmosis, while you're out playing dodge-the-rocks on your knob-bies. But *you* know all this stuff; you've been riding off-road for years.

The interesting thing, I thought, was that, expense aside (heh, heh), buying that mountain bike was painless. Well, you might say, why shouldn't it be painless? What's so awful about buying a new bicycle? Should be exciting, fun. Should be. But it isn't always, is it? Lots of us have been fooling with road bikes for years. We're sophisticated consumers, right? Me — I know too much for my own good. I fret at length about trifles that will make undetectable differences in my life.

I admit it: Buying a new road bike stopped being a pleasant, uncomplicated act a long time ago. And walking into a shop and picking one out — I'll take that blue one, thank you — no way. Unthinkable.

Not that I wouldn't like that blue one just fine; I probably would. I've spent too much time studying menus, ordering bicycles *à la carte*, conferring with the chef. And I'm far too conscious of the statement that each carefully chosen component, each frame detail, makes about my place in the cycling world.... I'm ruined for the new-bike quickie.

Buying the mountain bike, on the other hand, was casual and fun. It was easy. I knew just enough about off-road bikes to feel confident that a mass-produced bike would work out fine. And not enough, thankfully, to invent reasons why one wouldn't.

I'd already decided what brand I wanted. I dare not mention the name here, untainted as this space is by the scourge of brand favoritism. I'll disguise the name, and call it "Spanrock." You figure it out.

I wanted a Spanrock because I know Grant Petersen (not his real name), who designs them. A roadic for life, Petersen has a great attitude. He designs Spanrock bikes for *riders* — not for clipboard-toting comparison shoppers, or bikeside posers, but for men and women who'll actually get on and pedal the things.

Petersen knows all about bicycles, on-and off-road. He thinks (you can watch him do it) about bicycles obsessively, reflecting minutely on their mechanical, bio-mechanical and philosophical aspects.

I figured I'd let Petersen make the decisions, let *him* fret about component choices, angles, cable-routing and what-have-you.

I didn't want to *build* a bike, after all. I just wanted to own one, one I could feel fairly sure I'd like. I didn't want to spend weeks or days or even minutes educating myself about off-road hardware. No glamour there, no romance, to my mind. I just wanted something neat to ride.

I knew how much money I had. I knew what store I wanted to spend it in. I knew my size — almost for sure. I wasn't sure which model to choose; at the time, 1990 leftovers looked attractive, at slightly reduced prices. So did the '91s.

I went to the store. I asked the manager which Spanrock *he'd* buy, up to "so-much" money. He expected me to fuss over the decision, I think, so he generously gave me more information than I wanted. Hmmm.... I went to the racks of bikes and picked out a red one, a '91, the second Spanrock down from the top-of-the line MB-Zip (not its real name). I asked the mechanic to switch the brake cables to front-right (I'm an old motorcyclist), put on a pump and a bottle-cage, and to make sure the bike shifted okay — and he did. I wrote a check and the thing was done.

The feeling of relief was delicious. I owned a bike I did not have to give birth to without anesthetic. Maybe the whole mountain-bike program lends itself to lighter-heartedness. No harm in that; we could all benefit from a truckload or two of lightheartedness. Seriously.

I rode the bike the next day, and several times in the following week or so. I love that red bicycle and how it makes me feel; I've been caught giggling on it more than once. I'm glad I did just what I did.

There's something liberating (he wrote philosophically) about surrender. Granted (pun intended), I put myself in a win-win position. I knew the shop, I knew the brand, I had money earmarked to spend. All the alternatives were favorable. But none of that ever helped me in my "analysis-paralysis," road-bike past.

This time, though, I surrendered and emerged victorious. And lighthearted. I found somebody I could trust and trusted 'em.

See you on the trails. That guy under his bike over there on the ground, see, over by that big rock, the one giggling: That's me.

JUST SAY HI

Out there.... That's where I am: out there among you. While out there, I've noticed that some cyclists don't greet other cyclists coming the other way.

This column is for cyclists who don't say hi. If you do say hi, turn the page and read another story.

If you don't say hi, please write me care of my publisher and explain why you don't. I've knocked myself out trying to understand. Plop an intelligent individual, normally gracious and gregarious ("I'm a people person") onto a bicycle seat. Like magic, he or she goes brain-dead. You can watch the eyes go blank.

Help. Explain it to me.

I'll bet you said hi to everyone in the halls in school. I'll bet you felt rotten when someone hot failed to say hi back. After leaving school, you said hi to people for years. Then you started riding. And something about cycling turned you to looking straight ahead, ignoring other riders as if they were invisible. What happened?

Perhaps you're obsessed by the quest for the perfect training ride. You feel the road to fitness is hard and lonesome; you've got to walk it by yourself.

You feel that softening your focus long enough to greet another rider dilutes that cruel, solitary experience. Hey, you make cycling sound like big fun.

Maybe you don't say hi because you're concentrating on the road harder than most of us do. Something happened to you once. Maybe you rode over broken glass and got a flat. Maybe you hit a hole and bent a rim, or veered off the road and crashed. Is that it?

Maybe you sense that calamity could result from a moment's inattention. If that's it, don't be looking up and waving at me. Anything could happen, just from trying to be nice to me. Then I'd feel terrible.

If it's true, if you're concentrating hard all the time, every tedious mile, write and tell me so I won't feel bad when you don't say hi. Each mile will still last an eternity, though.

Maybe you feel you shouldn't speak to some cyclists, those who ride low-budget mountain bikes, or commute bikes with lights, or 10-speeds with visible brake cables. Or you go by clothing: You say hi to guys wearing no helmets or Giro helmets. You don't say hi to guys wearing Bell Bikers. You've got high standards.

Probably it takes you a while to rank oncoming riders on your personal scale. They're gone before you decide if you'll wave. I can relate; I don't make big decisions fast myself.

If that's the reason you don't say hi, decide if it's worth it to you in time and postage to send me a card explaining. If it is worth it, write me; I'll take a look at the card. Eventually. Your penmanship will count.

More seriously, someone suggested that people who don't say hi are car people. They're used to traveling in boxes, insulated from society by safety-glass and stamped steel. Covered up all the time.

Many new riders in the '90s buy a helmet and a pair of sunglasses before their first ride. So they're covered up on the bike, too. No wonder they feel as distant from life on that bike as they do in their cars. The experiences could seem so alike.

If they seem alike to you, try this. Next time you're out on your bike, reach over and crank down your window. Can't do it, can you? That's because when you're on your bike, you're not in your car.

This is your car on the interstate. That's your bike on the bike route. Any questions?

Perhaps, even after trying that experiment, you still won't be able to distinguish between bike and car. Further, you may not recognize that behavior appropriate in the one is not always appropriate on the other. If so, write me or call me on your car phone. We'll do lunch.

I'll explain over our lunch that some riders love how the bicycle keeps them reachable, how it doesn't erect barriers. Great opportunities can find them, they say, because the bicycle keeps them so accessible. Because the bicycle doesn't get in the way.

I believe they're right. And I believe they always say hi.

A SIGN

The road, wet from morning rain, curves up into the trees. Rom sits in the saddle, pedaling what looks like a low, easy gear. No traffic noise rises from the highway below. Rom listens, enjoying the quiet, enjoying hearing only the sound of his tires on the damp blacktop.

Behind him, the distant, angry whine of a geared-down engine intrudes. As he pedals, waiting near the white edge-line, the sound gets louder. It rises and falls in intensity as the driver slows for wet corners and accelerates between them.

He waits, listening, until the pick-up passes dangerously close to his elbow, surprising him. Red truck, wide wheels, guy driver, two women passengers. After passing him, the truck swerves uselessly away, oversize back tires losing grip and finding it again in a hissing tailwag.

One of the women turns her head and looks behind to see how the cyclist reacted to the near miss. Blank-faced, Rom gazes back at her; a heartbeat passes. She looks away.

"Back to the Metallica tape," he thinks. "What did she expect? That I'd scream and threaten, or panic and fall off my bike?"

How many times has that happened to me, he wonders. What's so offensive to those guys about bike riders? Is it just that they can push us around without worrying about us retaliating?

He wonders if studly, truck-drivin' dudes like this guy have ever been powerless, at the mercy, the way a cyclist is? Probably not, huh? Ought to take his truck away, make him ride a bike for a month or so, jack up his consciousness....

As he pedals, he can hear the guy's engine speed up and slow in the curves ahead. He knows the incident between him and the truck is over now, but he still feels a buzz from the sudden scare; from the adrenaline, whatever....

He wishes there could be more to the story, and a different ending: some triumph of the weak, some ... justice. He wishes he could know for sure there's a God. A God, he imagines, who deals with earthly inequalities; rights wrongs; makes sure the meek inherit — if not the *entire* earth — then merely a respected, bike-size parcel of it.

"You're being silly now, Rom," he says to himself outloud. "You just had one of the many close calls with cars or trucks you're bound to have if you ride the miles. Now you feel hurt and exposed; you're trying to invoke cosmic justice. Get real."

Lost in thought, he realizes he's heard the truck's engine-sound change, turn soprano. He hears an extended tire hiss — maybe two beats long — then quiet. He pedals up the hill, rounding wet, leaf-strewn corners. Quiet again now, he thinks. Nice.

He sees a guy and a woman standing on the right-hand roadside. The guy has his arm around the woman's shoulders. He recognizes the people from the truck. He sees that the guy is comforting the woman — but where the hell is the truck?

Rom sees the second woman climbing up the wet, grassy slope out of the gully. He sees the guy reach down to help her over the last bit of climb to the road's edge. Then he sees the red truck, down maybe 15 feet in the gully, right-side up and resting on a huge tree branch.

Rom resists the feeling that swells within him. He hears the sound of trumpets, the mingled voices of a choir. He feels guilty in the most delicious sense. But Rom is Rom; he does not gloat.

"Anything I can do to help?," he asks, pedaling very slowly.

"Yeah, get me somebody to help get my goddam truck back on the road," says the guy.

"Sure," says Rom, smiling, "happy to help."

Pedaling more briskly now, he goes off to find a park official. Locating one in moments, he tells him about the truck, waves goodbye, and resumes his ride.

Back on the curving, wet blacktop, Rom no longer yearns for proof that there is a force that rights earthly wrongs. At least for the moment, that search has been called off.

"No doubt about it," he says to himself, pedaling easily up the hill.

TO RIDE THE RIVER

I'm eating a calzone in a pizza place in Palo Alto with the Allsop guys: Mike Allsop, SoftRide sales manager Andy Ording, and racers Jim Sullivan and Alex Stieda. They're here promoting the SoftRide System, a high-tech beam that supports and suspends a bicycle saddle. I expect you've seen one or seen the ads by now.

The guys are visiting shops from Santa Barbara, a few hundred miles south from here, to Santa Rosa, maybe 60 miles north. They talk to shop people about the bikes and the SoftRide system. They ride on- and off-road with employees and customers, and, in one town at least, on the customary Saturday morning group ride.

Jim Sullivan is old, but he is fast. Sully is world vet mountain bike champion on points. Beat Albert Zwiefel, Sully did; first time anyone's done that.

Old as he is, Sully's never learned respect. He's smart, funny and irreverent clear to the bone. Got a pig valve in his heart. Really. Walk up and ask him. And Sully (he's my hero) has such a bad back, he claims, sponsorship or no, he can't ride anything but a SoftRide mountain bike. You could feel sorry for him if you didn't know how easily he could ride away from you.

If you can watch the old dude race, or talk with him somewhere, don't miss the chance. Or if you know some off-road racers who travel the circuit, ask them to tell you Sully stories. I bet they'll all know some good ones.

Alex Stieda is another hero of mine. New daddy Alex left wife Sam(antha) and daughter Kalie with family to go on the road helping the Allsops promote the beam. He's got a new 26-inch-wheel SoftRide road bike he'll ride in pro races all across the U.S. and Canada.

For those of you who don't go back in cycling, Alex was the first North American to wear yellow in the Tour ('86). He rode for 7-Eleven for years, and won lots of races.

I think Stieda must mean "class" in some language. You could sit around with racers and hear 100 Alex Stieda stories; all the stories would be about his unselfishness, his strength, his modesty. Hey, he's my hero.

So, where were we? Oh, yeah, it's Friday night. I'm sitting with my heroes, there in Palo Alto, on Ramona Street. We're eating these giant calzones. I get halfway through mine; I've had enough. I drop my fork. Sully's finishing his and staring across the table at my remaining half. Offers to help.

Hey, he needs the energy; the guys are driving to Sacramento early tomorrow morning to ride the Saturday "river ride." I ask what kind of ride they expect. It's flat, I add, and I've heard it's fast.

"I hope not," says Stieda, "I'd just like to go for a bike ride." "Me, too — probably have to hammer, though," says Sully, chewing and subtly shaking his head. Stieda nods, works on his calzone.

"Imagine this," I say. "Here you guys are. Probably one of you (fun to needle Sully) could go faster than anyone else on that ride tomorrow. And all you want to do is ride along and chat." They nod: That's exactly what they want to do.

"Who are those guys who want to go fast?" I ask. We try to figure that out for a moment. We decide they're not going to the Olympic Games or world's or reaching for a Bic to sign a pro contract. They're local guys whose passion is hammering on training rides.

We wonder if those guys are getting better at riding. We doubt it. We wonder if they're having fun riding. We doubt that, too.

I'm thinking as I watch Sully pound down my calzone, do those guys read the articles about how to get three weeks worth of fitness gain in one scientific, hour-and-a-half workout? Do they do hill intervals until they re-experience breakfast?

Do miles that go unrecorded on cyclometers or ungraphed by heart monitors even count? Instead of enjoying their riding, are these guys raising stress levels in already stressful lives by trying so hard to be fast?

I wonder if guys who take the sport so seriously will stay at it when the truth hits them. What'll they do when they stall at Cat III or even Cat II? When training articles, re-tasting breakfast, lifting weights and practicing water bottle science all fail to help?

I try to decide: Will they hang their bikes by the wheels in their garages and forget them? Will they tell friends at parties that, oh, yeah, they used to race bicycles? Lotta training. Lotta work.

Or will they wake up one morning and look out a window at sun-warmed empty streets and decide it might be fun to go for a bike ride? Alex and Sully and I'd be up for it. Call us.

STALE

Okay. If I tell you about this will you keep it between us two? Deal? Okay then, here it is: I feel really stale. This last couple of weeks, even though I'm up to my ears in cycling, I don't much want to ride my bike….

Does that amaze you? Can you believe I'd just admit it? Go ahead; break your promise. Call your buddies and tell 'em. I admitted in print that I have to force myself to hike my bottom onto the old Concor.

Try to understand. Take today — it's been raining out there all afternoon. Not that hard, but hard enough so I don't feel like getting out and maybe getting soaked. Just now you can see the sun trying to shine through the clouds. Chances are it'll quit raining, but even so it will probably take hours for the roads to dry off so my bike won't get all wet and gritty.

Yesterday it wasn't raining but it was cold. Kinda cold, anyway. I had an hour or so for a ride but I couldn't make up my mind which tights to wear. Single-front Lycra? Double-front? I went outside twice trying to decide. I still hadn't made an arm-warmer versus long-sleeve judgment when it got dark. Do I sound stale to you?

I never intend to get this way. It sneaks up on me. I wake up every morning thinking: Today's a great day to ride the bike. Most days I follow through on that thought; living here near San Francisco you can ride year-round if you don't mind a little rain. Could be that's the problem — our season's too long. Maybe if the weather forced me to take a winter lay-off I'd stay consistently eager through the spring and summer.

Or perhaps it's not *my* problem. It's society's problem. Americans are famous for short attention spans. We're almost immediately bored. Fads and styles come and go, selling us cures for boredom. But I never get bored with the concept of cycling:

It's climbing on the bike that's sometimes so difficult.

To make matters worse, I went to the Branders Tour of Texas and the Trump Tour this spring. You'd agree, I believe, that they're the two best international stage races on the U.S. calendar. I got to watch some of the finest bike racing in the world.

You'd think that would motivate me. You'd think I'd want to get skinny and super fit, want to stack up big miles. If you'd been there instead of me, seen all that top-level action, all those stars, you'd have come away totally motivated. Wouldn't you?

And I *do* get motivated. I sit on the airplane on the way home; I can't wait to get on my bike. But now I'm home feeling like someone let the air out of my tires. And stole my pump.

Speaking of those racing stars, how do you suppose they do it? Stay fresh, I mean. Pros spend at least four and sometimes seven or eight hours in the saddle per day, banking the miles in the early months.

Think how guilty one of those guys must feel if he gets stale. His job and his ability to come through for his teammates in races depend on his fitness. The whole team's counting on him. Can't be an easy responsibility to bear.

And some of those guys must live places where no other top-class riders live; they must have to put in big miles alone. Hard to stay excited, I'll bet. Would be for me.

If I could do all my rides with a pro team like 7-Eleven or Coors Light, burning up the roads in Sonoma County, California, in nice weather, I could set training records. I'd make the Olympic Training Team. But, alas, I have to ride the same old two or three local rides alone, or with my regular bunch of friends. We've all heard each other's stories. My friends never seem to complain. But I get stale.

Could I be overtrained? Physically burned out? No, not from 150 miles a week. Not much day-to-day stress, either. No, I have no convenient excuse.

I could deal more easily with my staleness guilt, I think, if I didn't feel so solitary about losing the excitement. Am I the only guy who gets this way? You never hear anyone talking about it.

Most guys will let you think they're tugging at the bit, counting the minutes until they can bolt from work, shed the tie and suit-up in Lycra. They can't wait to rush out and do big-gear hill intervals, two minutes on, 15 seconds off. Gotta hurt a little bit. Let off some steam.

Not me. The idea of rolling out solo on the same old road for the same old pain session fails to stimulate me. I don't look forward to solo rides. And practicing repeated, painful, unnatural fitness acts? No, not me, thank you. I just like to ride my bike.

I don't vary my routine enough. Probably that, too, has something to do with my occasional staleness. I wear more clothing in the winter to keep warm; I get a little fitter in the summer because I get in a few more miles. Hardly spice-of-life stuff. And what you'd laughably call my fitness program consists mostly of day rides with friends.

I must like it that way. I guess I just like the rides themselves. They're my goals — not merely steps on the way to building fitness for other, more important, rides.

And they're therapeutic, those conversational rides with friends. They're what I yearn for when I'm away. I want to come home and hop on my wonderful blue bike and meet about a dozen familiar, nearly perfect people, and spend a few calming athletic hours in their company. Out on the same old terrific roads we always ride.

Yup, it's therapy. Wait a minute; there's the sun. Hey, I think I've just got enough time to get a quick ride in. Thanks for listening. You've been great.

WHILE THEY WATCH

Or, You Fix your Flat on some God-forsaken Roadside while the Gang Waits

Shivering, the Sky Darkens and those First Drops start to Fall.

Abruptly, you realize that, for the first time — honestly — in months, you have a flat. As you slow and steer onto the shoulder, you remember to raise your arm; you yell, "flat," so folks will know. You stop your bike. Then, you climb off heavily and stand there a while. You stare at the problem wheel. You tell anyone who'll listen that you never, never have flats; you hate it when you do. You grumble in a low voice about the brand and model of tire, thankful you can remember them. No one else speaks.

Your complaints set the stage for an unfolding drama as your friends discover that you possess no flat-fixing hardware. No working pump, no spare tube, no patchkit, no tire levers. And why *should* you pack those things every ride; you never get flats. Damn pumps are always falling off anyway. Or mechanics forget to put 'em back when they take bikes off their repair stands. Or the washers inside dry out, like yours did.

You watch your friends eyes glaze as they catch on. They stand there in silence, weight on one leg, then the other, arms folded, hands buried in opposite armpits. Their breath makes big, cold-looking vapor clouds.

You've acted disgusted long enough. You remove the wheel from your bike. You inspect the tire for the guilty glass fragment or nail, turning the wheel around and around. You stall, afraid to admit you left your tire irons in your other jersey.

Someone hands you irons. You remove the tire and traitorous old tube from your rim. You look around helplessly. You remark, to no one in particular, that the glue in your patchkit dried up; you haven't had time to get down to Bob's and buy another.

You point out that you'd appreciate the loan of a tube, just to make the repair go faster. That way, you figure, you won't have to linger there so long, watching the expressions on your friends' faces change from impatient, to disgusted, to loathing, as you demonstrate your carelessness and ineptitude — while their sweaty undershirts freeze to their skin.

Someone, suddenly your best friend, silently hands you the new tube. It's as welcome as the sight of a beach party to a starving man adrift in a lifeboat. You borrow a pump from the same superstar and inflate the tube slightly. You're extra careful, wary of puncturing it here on this desolate roadside, 23 increasingly hostile men and women in attendance. You stuff the tube into the tire and work the bead into the rim most of the way around. Your cold-clumsy hands can't quite pop in the last of the bead, but you try, your breath fogging the wheel rim. You can hardly see as you work. Droplets condense on the frozen aluminum rim, running slowly, glistening, down the spokes. They freeze before they reach the first cross.

Someone pulls the wheel from your numb hands. As you watch helplessly, a 90-pound guy puts the heels of his incredibly thin, frail-looking hands, glowing cadaverous white from the cold, on the three inches of unmounted bead. Effortlessly, he snaps it into place in the rim. You mutter your thanks; he murmurs something you can't hear, and hands you the wheel.

You pick your bike up off the wet grass. Your chain has chosen today to fall off the rings and twist itself into a greasy, dewy-wet tangle. You paw at the snarled mess. Your hand, all its feeling gone, comes away anti-rust-coated for days. Especially under the nails — you're not going to corrode under there — no siree, not soon.

You beat at the nasty, kinked puzzle your chain has become, your hand a numb club from cold and frustration. You feel the bike tugged from your hands and watch as some frozen Samaritan touches a secret spot; your chain relaxes into its normal path, as if by magic. You breathe a vapor cloud of relief.

You pump the tire and remount the wheel in your frame. Miraculously, the tire slips unhindered between the brake blocks. The chain falls onto the small cog and hugs the big ring as you insert the wheel. The skewer tightens without fiddling. You snap the tire with a fingernail to check its pressure; it pings satisfyingly, but your frozen finger aches for two days from the shock. Even holding your hands under hot water, trying to scrub-brush away the chainlube packed under the nail, doesn't help.

Friday, you stop at Bob's on the way home from work. You buy a patch-kit and a pair of tire tools from Bob. He suggests you also buy a new tube to keep under your saddle. That'll speed up roadside repairs, he says; important if you're riding with other people.

Lots of folks carry several tubes, he tells you, especially on long rides. Something to think about. It's good, sometimes, to have an extra, Bob explains, in case someone else on the ride needs one.

As you leave Bob's, you decide some of this stuff might be worth considering. Maybe you'll get a tube or two when you buy the new pump, down the road. First time you hear they're on sale.

JUST NOD YOUR HEAD

Differences of opinion make life fun, someone once said. Was it young George Hincapie? Here are some opinions, formed in the white-hot crucible of my own riding and wrenching. Feel free to agree or disagree.

If you agree, I expect you will merely nod your head at my remarkable astuteness. If you disagree, do so on a comic postcard and mail it to me care of my publisher. Set me straight.

First, over the years I have developed a loathing for single-bolt seatposts, specifically micro-adjustable ones that have no "teeth" in the tilt adjustment to keep your saddle precisely level — the way you set it, the way God intended it.

I admit I present problems as a seatpost user. I push my saddle all the way back. I sit back on the seat when I climb. Though I weigh only 160 pounds, that's enough, it seems, to make some posts' tilt adjustments slip.

I have owned several of those seductive, treacherous gadgets, all prestige brands. I could name names, but doing so would cost me party invitations. I have loved unpacking them, admiring their satin or glossy anodized finishes. I have marveled at their lightness, at the silky precision of their tilt micro-adjustments. I have smeared expensive grease on them below their limit lines. I have gently coated the threads of their clamp bolts with that same glop and carefully installed the accursed, useless objects twixt bike and saddle; precisely measuring height and angle; firmly tightening binder and clamp bolt.

I have returned from rides of moderate duration and severity, new posts still glistening, my saddle tip intruding rudely into parts of my crotch that want, like Garbo, to be left alone. I have then, in tooth-grinding desperation, re-tightened those miserable inadequate bolts until they screamed for mercy. In return, they have caused *me* to scream — when they failed, painfully, infuriatingly, the very next ride.

If you, too, have had problems with single-bolt posts, please write and tell me. I can't be the only klutz in the world who can't make one work.

I still love two-bolt Campagnolo posts — *those* I can make work. You probably have a couple of discarded ones greying in your garage as you read this. People say they were too heavy, too clumsy to adjust, too much hassle. They did take a few minutes of fiddling — but only once.

Speaking of a few minutes of fiddling: I hate cantilever brakes. I have 'em on my mountain bike and my winter bike, but I haven't figured them out. Count, if you will, the ways you can adjust a modern cantilever. So many adjustments means so many ways to get it wrong.

I'm sure there are tricks I've never learned. My cantilevers are never "just right," nor do they feel as powerful as they should. Meanwhile, the Dia-Compe or Dura-Ace caliper brakes on my road bikes stop like mad and never need adjustment.

I love '90s shifting. I never have to look down at my cluster. My bike never decides it wasn't really in gear — so the chain never abruptly jumps down a cog. I do not have to "trim" the lever after shifting or tighten a 19th century wing-nut to tension my gear lever on climbs.

Thanks to eight speeds, I never need to change clusters to have all the ratios I need with no big gaps between them. Thanks to STI, I can shift anytime, even while standing up on pretty steep climbs. You don't do it every ride, but it's neat to know you can.

One of my bikes has (only) seven speeds and frame-mounted indexed levers. No problem — I could even go back to toe clips and lace-up shoes. But I'd resist returning to friction shifting.

Retro guys (they're all guys: The International Association of Retro Gals meets annually in a phone booth) who rave about friction shifting also recommend 25-year-old Jaguars as reliable transportation, "with a little fiddling." Right.

I like: fat clinchers ... nylon-lined, no-maintenance cable-housing ... Lycra bib-shorts with synthetic chamois ... membrane-thin wind jackets you can ball up and stuff in a jersey pocket ... polypro undershirts ... Oakley Frogskins ... Giro helmets. And discovering, about 25 miles into a ride, that you're really having *quite* a good day ... rides with awesomely strong, smart women like Janelle Parks, Kendra Kneeland or Sally Zack ... long climbs on narrow blacktop roads that corkscrew up through the trees ... the taste of strong coffee after a good ride with good friends.

I hate: inner tubes with valves so short your pump won't stay on them ... people who ride with tools rattling in under-seat bags ... Lycra clothing-snagging Velcro straps on gloves ... mountain-bike rides that were supposed to last two-and-a-half hours, but after three-and-a-half someone is saying, "let's see where *this* trail takes us."

I also hate: finishing the perfect tape-job and realizing I have a big, floppy loose section just behind a brake lever ... guys who preface equipment questions with, "I *know* it's in the legs but...," and virtually all bicycle-club business meetings.

And finally, I hate articles about the writer's pet peeves. Wasted space. Who cares?

SS396

It's a sun-warmed Friday afternoon in the hills above my home. I'm riding my motorcycle down a long, gentle grade on a curvy two-lane. The front of my BMW helmet is flipped up; I'm enjoying the warm air on my face.

I come up behind a grey primer Chevelle SS396 convertible, top down, three young guys in it. The guys are not, I figure, on their way to accordion lessons. Not in that muscle car.

In front of the guys is the reason I caught 'em — a man pedaling a 10-speed, helmeted head down, centered in the lane. I watch the Chevelle guys to see how they'll act, blocked by the cyclist. As I watch, they patiently drive 19 mph behind him (awright, dudes!) for a mile or two, then turn off. Now *I'm* behind him.

I ride up alongside on my motorcycle. I notice the mirror on his helmet. I wait until I'm sure he's not scared of me next to him and I say, "You know, there were three young guys in a primer Chevelle stuck behind you all the way down that last hill."

He says, "Hey, I was going the speed limit."

"Maybe so," I say, "but if I looked back and saw *those* guys in *that* car behind me, it'd strike fear into my heart. I'd move over."

He says he's got as much right out there on that road as they do, or as anybody does. I tell him I'm aware of that, I ride as many miles on a 10-speed as he does, probably. I say that I think, with due respect, that he's missing the point.

The point: Who cares who's right? Why get in the way of a car? Not just a car with macho-dude danger signs, but *any* car. Why do it? Why ask for trouble? Why not be considerate? Why not act the way you wish other people would act? Seems so elemental.

The guy with the 10-speed and the mirror says he'll watch out for primer Chevelles in the future. I think: This guy is unclear on the concept. Un-frigging-clear.

Then it's the next Wednesday morning. As I do most mornings, I read Herb Caen's column, the most popular part of the most widely read paper in northern California. Caen runs an item about a stretch limo, creeping along, caught behind an oblivious lane-hogging cyclist on a mountain road.

The limo follows the cyclist uphill for an eternity. Finally, one of the passengers, in a dinner jacket, stands up through the sunroof and pelts the cyclist with ice cubes from a champagne bucket. Rich people are awfully clever, don't you think?

The cyclist (I'm not making this up), ignoring the ice cubes, defiantly continues up the center of the lane, inexplicably, damnably, never-endingly ignorant.

Do you sense my frustration here? I know the guy in the limo acted stupidly, but he'll probably only harass one cyclist in his life. Who knows how many drivers the cyclist will annoy?

Hundreds of thousands, perhaps millions, of people read that column, chuckled at the madcap, ice-tossing Mr. Bigbucks and shook their heads at the typical uncaring cyclist. "Why are they like that?" For Northern California bike riders it was a PR disaster.

Whoever you are, pal, when you resolutely blocked the path of *that* limo, you did major harm to cyclists for hundreds of miles around. In 10 inconsiderate minutes you reinforced an already vivid negative stereotype in the minds of more people than populate many states.

My guess is you could care less. *You're* all right; nothing bad happened to *you*. All those other cyclists will just have to take care of themselves. Not your responsibility. On one level — your thick-headed, narrow, self-centered level — you're absolutely right.

But let's imagine what the highway world would be like if every cyclist behaved the same way you (and far too many others like you) do. What would it be like if all bike riders demanded the whole lane just as guys in Trans-Ams do? On the basis of, "Hey, I've got just as much right here as *anybody!*"

News would travel fast. There'd be a bounty on us by the weekend. Law enforcement would be helpless, palms up. Trans-Am guys would collect black shorts as pelts; they'd redeem them at participating convenience stores for 12-packs and pretzels on the eve of their annual festival, Super Bowl Sunday.

Don't be an idiot. Do what's best for *you* even if it's good for everyone else. Even if it's the right thing. When you hear cars comin' up behind you, get out of their way.

WIND

After the rest stop, 15 miles to go, a hot wind came up and blew in their faces. The route, scenic enough earlier, now took them through an old military base, block after block of cardboard-looking barracks long abandoned and condemned. Not much to see.

No doubt she was tiring. He didn't mind the riding in front, towing her in the heat and headwind. He could do it forever. But the miles had worn her down. Drafting him at 16 or 17 mph was beginning to be more than she could manage.

He'd look back, she'd be off his wheel. She'd grin: sorry, tried, couldn't do it. He'd wait, ride slower.

He thought about how often it happened that way. Late in the ride when the weaker partner was tired, a mountain would rise up or the wind would start to blow or a tire would go flat. Some straw would break the partnership's back.

They both knew she wasn't nearly as strong as he. She'd done a better job than either expected for nearly the whole ride. He knew she was dead game, that she'd hang if she possibly could, that she wouldn't give up. Hell, she wouldn't even stop smiling.

Nevertheless, as he waited, he felt himself becoming impatient, wondering guiltily if she truly was making an effort back there.

He felt himself growing tired of the century, ready for it to be over. He wanted a cold Coke, his helmet off and his back against a shade tree. He imagined the beads of condensation on the red can, the liquid rush of cool post-ride air in his nose and mouth, the feel of the grass on his stretched-out legs.

Riding slow now, waiting, he looked over his shoulder, saw her there five bike lengths behind, going nearly the same speed he was. She never dropped very far back but she couldn't quite keep it together to stay on his wheel.

He'd told her to think of his wheel as a lifeline. When you got a little tired or your concentration wandered, he'd said, and you came off that wheel, even for a moment, you had to spend big-time energy to get back on. Best plan is to stay on. She'd nodded as if she'd understood. But had she?

He moved over closer to the curb and eased off. She pedaled up alongside. How you doin'?, he asked. She smiled. Fine, she said, how're you feeling? I'm doing good, he said, you gettin' kinda tired?

Oh, my back hurts a little, she said, arching her back, holding the handlebar with her fingertips. And this ride sure gets boring the last few miles, huh? I remember from two years ago. Always have to ride through this army base. Boring.

Not too many more miles now, he said, sit in if you can.

But she couldn't. As he waited, he sank back into his thoughts. He could ride mile after mile at, say, 17 mph, into the wind. As long as she could sit on, she could ride that fast too. But the second she came off his wheel she could only ride maybe 11 or 12 mph, agonizingly slow in that heat and on that boring road. He caught himself calculating how much longer the last miles would take at her 11-mph pace than at his 17. He made himself stop before he lost respect for himself forever. Have to wash your mind out with soap, he told himself. When he checked behind, there she was, on the wheel.

At 13.5 mph, he made himself think about how she'd hung on behind him through the middle miles of the ride. He remembered how they'd rolled by surprised guys, guys down on aero' bars, guys in PDM jerseys, guys on carbon-fiber bikes with titanium saddles, guys with valuable high-tech water bottles, sometimes more than one.

They'd rolled by guys on flat sections, on long, gradual descents and on gentle upgrades. Passing guys was kind of a thrill, she'd admitted. I'll bet, he smiled.

At 13 mph, he remembered how she'd been reluctant to stay on the wheel at first, unused to trusting another person as her eyes. How she'd gotten more and more used to it as the miles passed, until, if she saw a hill ahead, she'd slip back there without him suggesting it, to save energy for the climb.

At 14 mph, with her on his wheel, he remembered how at first she'd lost time in corners, slowing down more than she had to, slipping out of the draft. Didn't take long for her to figure it out, though, and until she tired she'd hung in fine, better than fine.

He remembered all those things on the hot, boring suburban highway as he pedaled his bike 14 mph, monitoring her success on his wheel. He'd glance back; she'd grin, hanging on. Soon, maybe about the time he remembered how she'd learned to trust him in the corners, even the ones with a little gravel on them, he began to recognize the street they were riding on. He began to see cars with roof racks parked on both sides.

Just as he was considering how far she'd come since morning in skill and courage, he saw the high school parking lot where the century started and finished. Hey, he said, you did good. Wanna do another lap?

They rolled in side by side, flopped the bikes down in the grass, in the speckled shade of a big tree. I'll sign us in, he said; you relax. He checked them in, pocketed their patches, filled their bottles with cold water, grabbed a napkinful of miniature chocolate chip cookies and two bananas and found the soft drink machine. Bought two cans.

Didn't take him more than five minutes to do it all. She was still smiling when he sat down under the tree, spread open the napkin full of cookies, opened both cans, grinned and handed her hers.

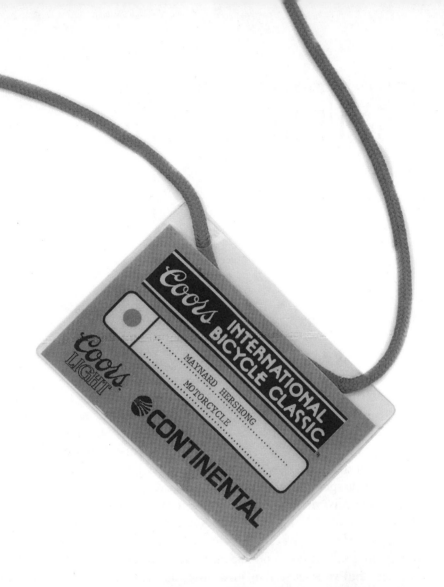

RETRO

RIDERS OF THE LOST ART

I got to thinking today about forgotten bike-rider rituals — like reaching down to tighten toe straps, thereby telegraphing to one and all that you were primed to sprint.

Or the practice of removing inner brake cables to grease them so they wouldn't rust inside the old (unlined) housings. Campy brakes came along in '69 with cable anchors that didn't kink cables the way other brakes always had. Your cables would last forever if you removed them from time to time for maintenance.

Further reflection (had to brush cobwebs out of my reflector) reminded me how many of our rituals sprung from the trials of sew-up tires. I don't ride sew-ups anymore and I don't miss them, but there was a feeling of kinship among us bikies brought about, perhaps, by mutual suffering under their tyranny. Tyre-anny....

As you may know, you would carry a spare tire, one that had been used but remained (you hoped) airtight, folded in a bundle under your seat. Other tires came and went (boy, did they), but your spare remained inviolate, serving only to get you home. Otherwise it stayed stored under your saddle rails.

If you were aware of the custom and cared about such things, your spare spent its underseat life protectively wrapped in several folded yellowing pages of *Competitive Cycling* or *L'Equipe* newsprint.

You cinched it, thus wrapped, under your saddle with a worn-but-not-tattered beige Binda Extra toe strap, never some cheap red Christophe liberated from a Peugeot UO-8. Nay.

When you flatted, you stripped the flat tubular off the rim, stretched on and pumped up your spare. Once home, you pulled the spare off the wheel and laboriously cemented a new or repaired (rarely) tire, generally of dubious quality, onto the rim.

You threw today's flat tire atop a repulsive, expensive, deepening graveyard mound of perished tires. You intended to fix them, really you did, but meanwhile you stashed them on "your" closet floor, out of your girlfriend's sight.

Last, you refolded your faithful spare into a compact, tread-out bundle, wrapped it in that old *Competitive Cycling* and strapped it back under your worn #3 Cinelli saddle. Done.

That ritual — folding a spare sew-up — struck me as significant. It was a tradition taught to you by a cycling elder, a ceremony bike riders shared in those primitive cycling days, days that glow in the memories of so many of us.

It *was* a sort of initiation: When you saw the occasional dorky rider, his brand-new, clumsily folded spare gave him away nearly as dramatically as his crazily tilted saddle, white legs and mid-calf, black socks.

Someone older and wiser in cycling told me long ago that wherever you went — Poland, Peru or Pittsburgh — bikies folded their spares the same way. So? Back then, trust me, that knowledge comforted us.

We knew next to nothing, remember, about riding or racing outside our backwater ABLA or USCF world. Books and magazines offering exotic cycling lore were scarce or nonexistent, TV coverage unimaginable.

So if we could conclude — on the scant evidence of a universal style of spare bundling — that a bike rider was a bike rider anywhere, *every*where, that conclusion comforted us. We could feel part of something real, a fraternity that transcended borders, culture and language.

Today, we know everything about cycling everywhere. Cycling magazines and newspapers tell us about riding in China, in Italy, in Colombia. You can watch the Tour on TV most years, and buy dozens of books and videos. Not nearly as much mystery today.

Today's bikes are virtually idiot-proof. You don't have to read articles or watch videos or sit at the feet of a master to learn how to maintain your bike. After all, bike riders want convenience, not arcane maintenance lore, messy tire glue, and charming hardships out of horse-and-buggy days.

And they get convenience: Bikes offer painless 20th century technology. Everything clicks. Everything's easy but the pedaling. That part hasn't changed.

You no longer ask a shoemaker to nail on your cleats. You don't tighten your shift lever at the bottoms of hills. You don't reach down to cinch up toe straps. You don't smear evil, hospital-smelling, softening glop on your stiffening chamois.

You don't glue on your tires. You don't have a burial mound of sad, failed sew-ups hidden away. You don't learn to fold your spare the way riders in Portugal fold theirs.

Easier's easier, no argument. Better? Better's more complicated, something else again. We'll talk about better on a ride sometime. Tomorrow? Hey, tomorrow's good for me.

IN ONE ERA, OUT THE OTHER

At the 1988 Reno bicycle trade show, if you stood in just the right spot, you could see into two eras. From right in front of the little Hetchins booth, you could see both the one Hetchins frame and the big splashy Screamin' Eagle frame booth across the way.

You did not have to elbow through a crowd of oohers and aahers to admire the Hetchins. Across the aisle, on the other hand, the Screamin' Eagle booth was jammed with people talking business. High-tech Screamin' Eagle business is good; Hetchins-style business, I believe, is quieter, thus this article.

Hetchins bicycles could only be English. They are emblems of a prouder British past, when that nation was an industrial giant and craftsmanship was in flower. A Hetchins frame represents hours of painstaking hand construction by the builder himself. The man whose name is on the frame built it. That's an old fashioned-sounding idea today, isn't it?

The Hetchins frame model that's become most famous (known to several dozen people in the U.S.) is the "curly-stay," characterized by gracefully bowed seat — and chainstays. In 1988, those curved frametubes look antique and quaint, but still lovely.

Hetchins frames have curved tubes because back a few decades, the rules governing bicycle racing in England prohibited framemaker decals. Officials thought that advertising on the bikes tainted the pure amateur sport. But builders wanted readers of *Cycling*, the weekly paper, to be able to spot their products in race photos. They developed personal frame designs fans could identify without decals. They used such curiosities as curly rear triangles, funny-shaped forks and seat stays that joined the top tub inches in front of the seat cluster. Charming stuff.

Hetchins frames are available in several grades, varying in the fantastic detailwork. Most Hetchins that reach the U.S. feature incredibly ornate hand-cut lugs and fork crowns. The filagreed fork crown trim often extends a couple of inches down the blades.

The bottom-bracket tangs and brake-bridge trim could be equally fancy. Someone very skilled spends hours and hours fashioning those lugs and crowns, probably someone named Hetchin. The frameset I saw at the Reno show had it all. Gee it was beautiful.

Across the aisle, surrounded by nice '80s folks, was the new-as-tomorrow Screamin' Eagle, computer-designed, made of something or other from aerospace research and looking ever so sleek and state-of-the-art. I didn't ask anybody, because I was in no position to act on the answer, but I'll bet the price of the Hetchins and the Screamin' Eagle are close to the same.

I'll also bet that curvaceous new Screamin' Eagle is great to ride. I'm willing to believe claims that it flexes not at all in the vicinity of the bottom bracket. I'll concede that it has chainstays that could strike awe in the hearts of bridge abutments in the area of rigidity.

I'll even admit that the one-piece look might grow on an owner, that he or she might, in time, get to like it. I'll even go along with test reports that the pricey device combines track-bike stiffness with boulevard ride. I still don't want one.

But perhaps you do. And perhaps you're in a position to afford one. There are lots of reasons to buy a bike like one of those and there'll be lots of encouraging, admiring voices. Here's a tiny note of dissension from a guy who would never claim to be objective. My argument is entirely emotional. There's nothing the matter with those bikes.

When you buy a Hetchins, or a Serotta, or a DeRosa, or a U.S. Terry, you are paying for hand assembly of known components. You are paying for a certain number of hours spent by an artisan who, in many cases, has *you* in mind. The frames cost good money because tube sets and lugs and hours of a craftsperson's time cost good money.

Perhaps the first Screamin' Eagle, or the first 1000 Screamin' Eagles, will be expensive to produce. Soon, however, economies of scale and the reduced need for skilled hand labor will bring the cost down, first to the builder, then to the eventual customer. High-tech will become everyday. There will be Screamin' Eagle clones available at hardware stores.

Let's say you buy one of the new Screamin' Eagles, let's call it model One. A component of your desire for that frame will be its stature as the Latest Thing. Sadly, a year from now or a month from now, those rascally Screamin' Eagle constructors will unveil model Two, and perhaps Three, the deluxe version with all the glue-ons. Your bike will ride just as well, but it will have lost its "ultimacy." Has to happen. Part of what you paid for has vanished.

Every Hetchins ever sold remains a source of pride to its owner. So does every DeRosa, every Serotta. Truly handmade bikes will never flood the market, because craftspersons' hands can only work so fast. And a year-old Eisentraut loses nothing, in real or perceived value.

Because bicycles are so perfected, because they do not have motors, because they can only do what you are able to cause them to do, there are only tiny differences between the dozens of good ones. By opting for the latest, trickest thing you set yourself up for eventual dissatisfaction. It's never the latest for long.

And the truth is: if you and your buddy go to the races, you on your new-as-*now* monument to far-seeing science and your friend on stronger and smarter will win. That's a wonderful aspect of cycling, and it's an aspect some people would prefer you forgot. Long enough for your credit card approval to light up the screen.

VIVID FLASHBACKS

I used to wear wool shorts. S'true. Worse, I resisted trying Lycra shorts the first few years they were around. Disco shorts, I called them. Why, you can tell a man's religion from across the street in those things, I said.

I figured Lycra would come and go like disco did. So I soldiered on in Italian or U.S.-made, black, 100-percent virgin wool shorts with genuine deerskin chamois. That's what we discriminating cyclists wore in the years of our collective ignorance.

If you think about what bike shorts do, you will realize those wool shorts did it all really badly. What should cycling shorts do? They should cover your nakedness. They should warm your thighs. They should hold an absorbent, friction-reducing pad smoothly against your butt. That's all.

And what did wool shorts do? Wool shorts covered your body, but not well. They were okay when they were new, or dry, but soon as they stretched (which took 6.3 miles), or got wet, the legs rode up, and the waists and butts sagged down. In the rain, your shorts held more water than your bottle.

Yes, you could wear suspenders and keep the waist where you wanted it. But nothing would keep the legs down near your knees, warming your thighs and looking like Gimondi's did in team photos. Team photos were taken on dry days and short rides. Look at Gimondi in an old Tour shot: wool legs bunched up, his shorts looking like a bathing suit.

We agreed cycling shorts should hold a pad smooth against your bottom, right? Alas, wool shorts stretched unevenly as you rode. Once they stretched, they bagged and wrinkled in the seat — that critical area between tender skin and saddle. Lamentably, the chamois sewn inside wrinkled too.

So, after a few short miles, there you sat — on a sweaty, salty, bacteria-ridden piece of wrinkled deerskin. The good old days. If you were lucky, the wrinkled deerskin pinched and chafed your tender butt-skin, raising minor, forgettable welts. If you were *not* lucky, the wrinkled deerskin caused — in that warm and disgusting environment — the formation of major, painful, debilitating saddle boils. They took days to go away, usually days off the bike. Almost everyone got 'em, one time or another. Bike-mag articles regularly suggested cures, some nearly voodoo-mystical. Sometimes a doctor had to lance (gross!) them to relieve the pain and pressure. Saddle boils were a pre-Lycra big deal.

Ah, but the wrinkling wasn't the worst of it. The shorts and chamois were natural materials. They were sensitive. No way could you care for them casually or roughly like crummy synthetics. No machines. No convenience. No way. You cleansed your wool shorts by hand, in a sink with Woolite and cold water. You washed them gently, careful not to wring them or scrub them vigorously. Then you rinsed them over and over until you could no longer stand to do so. You gently squeezed the water from them and set them aside to air-dry, out of the rays of the awful old, destructive sun. So, they never got clean and they never got sanitary.

Just the perpetual nastiness would've been bad enough - but even the cold-water-and-two-days-to-dry ordeal didn't keep the chamois from losing its suppleness shockingly quickly. Two or three washings and that proud piece of delicate, genuine leather looked and felt like something you'd use with a belt-sander to finish furniture. So, you'd re-soften the chamois with something you thought might work: some evil-smelling, ludicrously expensive, commercial chamois preparation; Noxema, Vaseline — anything — so you could wear your nearly-new shorts again. Oh, that slime felt excellent against your butt on a cold race morning.

Worst, though, worst by far, was when you dressed while hiding behind your car door before the race. As you pulled on your shorts, without your realizing it, the chamois sometimes brushed the ground. Bits of local geology adhered to the greasy, carefully softened chamois. Ah but, it's important — in sport — to learn to suffer, no? Builds the character, no?

Racing in wool shorts was distasteful enough. *Touring* in them was worse. Consider this: If you have to hand wash your shorts and they take two days to dry, how many pairs will you need on a 10-day, dawn-to-dusk tour? How will you carry the Woolite? The Noxema? The wet shorts? How many days straight will you try to wear each pair? How many saddle sores can you develop in one tour? How tough are you?

I remember that after a year or so in Lycra, I'd put wool shorts behind me (so to speak). In my soul, I wanted never to see a pair again, afraid the sight might provoke vivid, disturbing flashbacks.

But I still own some really special ones — scarcely worn Moas and Vittore Giannis, exotic European company names beautifully embroidered down the legs. I once threw them in a box and took them to a parts swap at a club meeting. Offered them for sale at what I thought was a fair price. Something like, uh, nothing. No takers.

No wonder.

THE OLD DAYS

Even though Bridgestone is no longer with us as a company, the old "B.O.B. Gazette" — the Bridgestone Owner's Bunch newsletter — is still being published. They once ran the question, "Why you would like a B.O.B. fanny pack." And since Bridgestone must have been the most retro major bike-maker around, I wrote my answer in this retro-style poem.

GOOD ENOUGH FOR FAUSTO, BY BOB 450

> Would I like the old days back?
> Will I ride my inch-pitch hack
> Till they bring the Yardbirds back?
> Do I love my Pletcher rack?
> 5   And do I want the old days back?
> By Bianchi green - I do.
>
> Do I like my Dettos black?
> Am I tattooed (twice) "Mafac?"
> Will I ride my early Sachs
> 10   Till the paneled downtube cracks?
> So do I want the old days back?
> By Kelly's clips— I do.

2 Inch-pitch — old chain-and-sprocket tooth-spacing
4 Pletcher rack — the old standard (pre-Blackburn) in luggage racks
7 Dettos — Detto Pietro shoes: popular, old, low-priced shoe
8 Mafac — French manufacturer of brakes

9 Sachs — Richard Sachs bicycles, made in Connecticut; fine, old-fashioned, hand-crafted bikes with paneled downtube, painted like an old British frame
12 Kelly's clips — Sean Kelly used toeclips years after everyone else in the pro ranks switched to clipless

Am I put off by Kestrel's act?
Do I take the Coni book as fact?
15   Will I ride 40 holes in back
Till proper wooden rims come back?
Do I want the old days back?
On Gino's health I do.

Do I defend, face-to-face,
20   Merckx's "real-bike" hour pace?
Do my shifters clamp in place?
Do I forget I never raced, just
Ground along at tourist pace
But passed by women, always chased?
25   But do I want Dura-Ace erased?
Trust me; yes, I do.

In my world, shorts would all be black,
All young guys would ride the track,
And fix my silks at a buck a crack.
30   See, I speak Campy, but my voice is cracked,
I'm clipped and strapped, but I'm off the back,
I learned the lingo, but forgot the knack,
I'm retro-suffering in the laughing pack.
Getting dropped is what I do.

35   Enough already with the sordid facts;
I've admitted I want the old days back:
Like a red Bob Jackson in Santa's pack,
Beige-box pieces, front to back.
Cinelli, Bindas, S.L. blacks,
40   Each thread lubed with warm beeswax.
We love our dreams but we live by facts;
I'd settle for a BOB-club fanny pack.

---

13 Kestrel — high-tech, non-retro bicycles
14 Coni — the old Italian Federation training bible
15 40 holes — old, super-strong wheels used 40 spokes
16 wooden rims — either wood, or wood-filled aluminum rims
18 Gino — Gino Bartali, Coppi's rival in the '40s and '50s
20 "real-bike" hour-pace — Eddy Merckx's hour record was the last set on a conventional bicycle
21 shifters clamp in place — before braze-ons
29 silks — expensive sew-up tires

33 laughing pack — the chatty group that has given up trying to be competitive in the race but is trying to finish within the time limit
37 Bob Jackson — well-known British builder
38 beige-box pieces — old Campy parts came in beige boxes that many of us saved
39 Bindas — Alfredo Binda toestraps, the best old straps
S.L. blacks — black-caged Superleggera pedals which many of us rode
40 warm beeswax — Bridgestone's Grant Petersen's recommendation for thread lubrication

ON
RACING

TOUR MYSTERY

"Yo Ralph, it's Jimmy. Did ya watch the Tour on TV?"

"Yes, just turned it off. Pretty neat for Bauer, huh, the Canadian guy."

"Oh, yeah, it's great for Bauer and 7-Eleven. Second time he's worn yellow in the Tour. Whattaguy."

"I have to say, Jimmy, I'm not sure I understand all I saw today. Maybe you could explain it to me."

"Hey, sure, Ralph. What do you wanna know?"

"Well, I could see why they spent so much time showing us the first stage. I guess it wasn't *really* the first stage, even though it seemed like it should be. The prologue, right?"

"Right."

"Well, as I say, I could see why they took the time showing that prologue 'cause it split the guys up a little; I know a few seconds matter a lot, even in a long race. You told me about last year, remember. The eight seconds."

"Uh-huh."

"Well, I watched those guys riding with funny handlebars and solid wheels to save the few seconds. Then the TV people interviewed the guy with the curly hair, the guy who invented the funny handlebars. He seemed kinda embarrassed that some folks thought his bars had won, last year, for Greg. The bars only evened it up, he claimed, for Greg having a crummy team last year.

"What I mean: You'd have thought he'd be prouder. If I'd invented handlebars ugly as those that everyone bought anyway, I'd be proud. Hey, you don't just see 'em on racers' bikes on TV; you see 'em out here on the bike path that runs past my house."

"Right, Ralph. Anywhere seconds count."

"So, knowing that seconds *do* count, I was kinda surprised when those four guys got 30 seconds away. But I figured, whenever the pack wants to catch 'em, they will. Right?"

"Right. Well, usually."

"Then, the four guys got further and further away. They got 12 minutes away. Hey, they stayed 10 minutes ahead clear to the finish. You've got to explain that to me. Didn't you tell me Delgado lost a couple minutes getting to his start late, last year?"

"That's right. Then he lost more time because he was still upset in the following team time trial."

"Well, he didn't blow any 10 minutes *last* year, did he? And didn't you tell me that the couple of minutes he *did* blow maybe cost him the Tour?"

"Right, I did say that was possible."

"And Fignon lost the whole Tour by eight seconds on the last day, maybe because he didn't wear his helmet or put on the curly-headed guy's ugly bars?"

"Right again."

"Well, then why did the big group let those four guys get so far away today? How can they expect to make up 10 minutes on four pretty-strong guys?"

"Several reasons. Some of those guys knew they had to ride another stage, a team time trial, that afternoon; that might've de-motivated 'em to chase. And four teams had riders in that four-man break, so those teams wouldn't chase.

"The rest, maybe they figured there wasn't a Tour winner in that four, no real contenders. Who knows, maybe they were right. We won't know until the mountains."

"Can't Steve Bauer climb mountains?"

"Sure he can. He's a pretty high-rated all-around rider. He's not a natural climber, but he can hang in."

"Strange they'd let him get so far ahead. And LeMond's teammate — what's his name — Pensec, isn't he a good rider? Why did LeMond say that he thought it was good for him having Pensec so far ahead?"

"Well, with a rider from his team so far ahead overall, LeMond and the 'Z' guys won't attack, nor will the other three guys' teams. They'll rest and wait for teams that don't have riders leading to make the effort. Then they'll tag along."

"Oh, I'm starting to understand. But can LeMond take that kind of chance? What if Pensec steals the race? You told me LeMond makes more money than anyone else. Can he justify taking that much money for supporting a guy who makes a fraction of what he does?"

"No, I don't suppose he can, Ralph. But, again, the mountains will probably take care of that. Pensec is not known to be such a great climber. If he tries to keep up with the best guys on the long grades, he may blow up and lose big chunks of time — so much time that the 10 minutes will seem like nothing."

"Then why did he break away in the first place, Jim? Why would he waste the effort? He could just sit in and try to save energy for the mountains, to try to do the best he could on the climbs."

"See, Ralph, you forget that the Tour gets hours of live coverage on European TV. The sponsors are delighted when a rider gets his face and jersey on the screen for some of those hours.

"And a Tour de France stage win, even for a flat stage that doesn't change the overall standings, is a big deal for a rider and his team. Sometimes, a guy won't even intend to finish the whole Tour; he'll try to win a sprint finish early on; then he'll quit.

"Or he'll try to finish the mountain stages barely under the time limit for disqualification. Guys like that race the Tour for the flat stages, for sprint points. Other guys will try to get to the tops of mountains first, for those points. Different guys have different aspirations."

"How come the TV commentators don't tell us all this stuff?"

"Ralph, I bet they think they'd just lose you. They figure the audience isn't aware of the subtleties and won't bother to become aware. Like soccer, probably. Cycling and soccer demand a pretty sophisticated fan."

"You know, Jim, I can see this could be a problem. Where would I have found out about all this stuff if I couldn't call you? And will people who can't figure out what's going on keep watching? There was a pretty good James Caan movie on the other channel I could've watched without any background at all."

"Happy to help. Call me any time."

"You bet. Talk to you after next week's coverage."

VIP

I joined the Branders Jeans Tour of Texas in Kerrville, in Texas's beautiful, sparsely populated Hill Country.

At the Branders Tour, we had first-class bicycle road racing on wide, smooth, rolling roads. We had 80 or 90 women and almost twice as many men. We had Olympic and national champions, 7-Eleven, Coors Light, Soviets, Czechs, teams from all over the world.

We had competition so close a four-second lead opened in the prologue won the Tour hundreds of race-miles later. But we had no fans at the road races. No, we had *one* fan.

My first day there, technical director Mike Nix and I drove in front of the women's race. Three times on the 52-mile Bandera-Leakey course, we saw an old guy in Team Wolverine clothing riding along, watching the race go by.

Nix and I waved and honked our horn when we saw him. He'd grin and wave back, evidently having a great time. At the finish, there he was again, a tanned, skinny, fit-looking old guy decked out in Wolverine team stuff. He'd cruise around the start-finish area on his mountain bike, watching the action and smiling at folks.

He wasn't officially involved with the race, I decided, just a spectator. A fan. But a Wolverine? Here?

The Wolverines hail from Detroit, Michigan, distant geographically and culturally from Kerrville. The fine old Wolverine club has produced a remarkable number of champions. Young Wolverines get coaching other riders can only dream about.

But our far-from-home fan was no young Wolverine. He looked about 60, I'd say, an athletic 60. He knew how to ride, too. He had style, even on his mountain bike.

After the race, I heard people talking about the old guy. On those lovely, empty, Hill Country roads, you notice anything that moves — especially a bike rider wearing clothing from a club 1000 or so miles away. Everyone saw him.

At a post-race banquet in Kerrville, I saw him again, sitting alone, eating at a long picnic table. I went over and sat down, asked him how he was doing.

I learned he was indeed from Detroit, that he was using part of his vacation to follow the Branders Tour. I learned how proud he was of his club and its history. He contributed articles to the club newsletter, he told me. T.J. Hill, his name was, and he'd been riding and racing bikes since 1947. *Nineteen forty-seven.* Imagine.

T.J. and I and a few friends sat over pasta, then dessert and coffee. We heard stories about cycling back before anyone I know rode a bike.

T.J. told us about Mike Walden, the respected Wolverine coach, and one famous Wolverine rider after another. He described rides in virtually every state, climbs over every brutal hill. He told stories from thousands of miles of cycling, some dating back decades. I wish you could've been there.

Next morning, I talked with David and Drew Mayer-Oakes, the brother team who, with Richard DeGarmo, run the Branders Tour. We got T.J. a VIP pass. We put him in a seat Len Pettyjohn offered in his Coors Light team car.

The ride with Pettyjohn put an even wider smile on T.J.'s face. He'd never seen a race from inside except from the saddle of his bike. He'd never been inside anything like the Branders Tour.

Each road race, we put him in a team or official car so he could get the insider view. We put him on motorcycles at the last two events on closed courses. There, the motorcycles stay busy giving VIP rides, getting "important" people close to the action.

So T.J. rode on a VIP motorcycle at the circuit race in Round Rock and at the downtown Fort Worth criterium. Hundreds of Texas fans smiled as the fit-looking, tan man from Michigan grinned at them from Johnny Kresena's BMW sidecar, circling the course.

The Branders Tour brought many important cycling people to Texas that spring. Most got VIP treatment from the race and the local people.

Because so many Texas people will see this and so few will get to read the Wolverine club newsletter, I'd like to thank the folks of Texas and the Branders Tour for taking such good care of T.J. and the rest of us … for treating all of us like VIPs.

Especially T.J. Hill, Wolverine, from Detroit, Michigan, the Branders Tour of Texas's most important "Very Important Person." If you ask me.

EASY DAY

I took my bike up to Santa Rosa, California, toward the end of January, for a visit at the 7-Eleven training camp and a ride or two with the guys. And once there, I maintained a veneer of cool assurance for all to see. Totally casual, I faked confidence that I could hang with the boys on the Sonoma County hills, and could finish pro-length training rides without CPR or oxygen-support apparatus.

Last January, I visited the Coors Light camp and rode with that team, including the pre-comeback Greg LeMond. But I did not survive long on my ride with the Coors Light guys. LeMond, happy to be on his bike and with his (U.S.) team, evidently felt frisky. He went right to the front and dropped — what I would call — the hammer. In pitifully few uphill moments, I went out the back. As rumor has it, I wasn't the only casualty on that ride; far better men than I watched helplessly, as the back of that pack got progressively smaller in the distance.

This time, though, I resolved things would be different. I put in my usual maybe 150 miles per week through the fall and winter. I rode the 63-inch fixed gear up and down the East Bay hills, building strength and leg-speed, and raising my hammer index.

I rode club training rides and often did not get dropped. I raced three, freezing-cold, wet miles up San Bruno Mountain, near San Francisco, on New Year's morning and finished the same day I started. Hey, guys like me call that fitness.

I doubted, however, that the men on the 7-Eleven pro racing team would call that fitness. But it was all I had, so at 10 o'clock Tuesday morning, January 22, I walked my bike out past the poolside mechanics' area to roll out on an "easy day" with the guys.

Yes, with Steve Bauer, Urs Zimmermann, Sean Yates, Davis Phinney, Andy Hampsten ... about 20, total. Twenty guys everyone's heard of. Twenty guys whose photos you see in magazines; snarling, baring their teeth as they contest mountaintop stage-finishes. And *me*, aging columnist, X-ray photos of whose bared teeth you may someday see featured in *Dental Disasters Magazine*.

An easy day for the Slurpies is four hours. Hard days are seven or eight hours. Don't ask me about the hard days; I did not have the nerve to hop on my bike at 10 a.m. with 20 lean guys dressed in green, white and red — all on new Eddy Merckxs — knowing I wouldn't be hopping (hah) off until 5 o'clock in the afternoon.

Training-ride speeds are high, but not godawful hard. I suppose none of the guys felt he had anything to prove. The pace and the manner of riding were so smooth (Slurpie smooth). The perceived effort felt constant over the hours. We rode between, say, 18 and 23 mph over the beautiful, rolling Sonoma County roads; just me and most of the 7-Eleven Professional Racing Team.

Sitting in that bunch is like traveling first-class on the finest express train. It's what you've always wanted from a bike ride but were afraid to ask for. Go ahead, I understand perfectly: Stop reading and eat your heart out. You can finish the story later.

We rode in a two-abreast pace line, the front two taking long, easy pulls, and sometimes sitting up there for miles at a time. We rolled out in the big ring, and mostly stayed in the big ring except for several steepish climbs that had guys out of their saddles. Had them standing up, but not hammering — not on an easy day — but climbing fast enough to have *me* breathing hard.

Once, near the top of one of those hills (maybe I dreamed this — but it seems real), Bob Roll pushed me a little when I'd drifted back. Got me back on. Just the once.

Mostly I sat in that big group and felt totally confident: All was well. No one was about to fall down, or get surprised, or do anything foolish. I liked that feeling. I started to get used to the speed and the steady, mile-eating pace. My legs felt loose, warm and strong; they liked it. I realized I was smiling.

The roads we covered were flatter than those around my home; I could sit in the saddle and turn the 17 or 15. I began to feel good, *racing* good. I looked up the line of men, at Alex Stieda, Steve Bauer, Nathan Dahlberg and Jeff Pierce.

How bad *is* this, I thought to myself. So I asked Nathan Dahlberg, "Nathan, how bad is this?" He said he felt that riding those scenic byways in the company of almost two-dozen agreeable guys — and getting paid for it — was not so bad, really. Not terrible. Those New Zealanders understate everything.

I tried to remember that in a few weeks, these guys would have to suffer; earning their pay in cold, wet, early-season racing. Maybe some of them would wonder, then, if it was worth it. Maybe the guys for whom form was slow in coming, or who got sick, or who simply haven't the talent some of the others have — maybe they'd wonder if it was worth it. But I couldn't keep myself concentrating on what was going to be happening later, after the training camp broke up, and the guys packed up their bikes and flew away to wherever Och had decided they belonged next.

I couldn't keep myself from thinking that I was riding that perfect road with the finest American team of racing cyclists ever assembled. And some of the finest guys. I looked over at Urs Zimmermann, knowing Urs was happy as he could be to have joined 7-Eleven, happy to be left alone, some days, to ride off by himself for eight or nine hours. Happy simply to be here.

Zimmermann and I had chatted for a mile or so, back a ways, about journalists, and Swiss and American people, traffic — stuff bike riders talk about. *You* know. His English is just okay so far, and I don't speak any of the other four or five languages he speaks. So conversation's kind of an effort.

But not *all* conversation. I looked over at Zimmermann, his handlebar inches from mine as we rolled along on the "easy day." I took my hand off my bar and made a gesture, sweeping my arm up and across the scene as if to say, "look at all this. Isn't it wonderful?"

Urs Zimmerman grinned at me in all languages and no language at all —"It is."

SPECIAL TREATMENT

I saw a rider ahead of me on the hill and picked up my pace, thinking it would be good to have company on my ride. The rider turned out to be a woman, going as fast as I'd ever go by myself. I had to pedal extra hard for a half-mile to catch her; I rode alongside and gasped my hi.

"Hi", she said back. "How're you doing," I asked. "Oh, not too well," she said, with a little self-deprecating, I'm-so-slow-it's-laughable laugh; "I'm just out for a short ride at lunchtime".

Maybe *she* thought she was slow, but trying to keep pace with her and chat was all I could do.

"Oh, a Lighthouse," she said, looking at my bike, "I've heard of those." "What'd you hear," I asked. "Oh, just that Maynard Hershon has one." "Uh, you aren't Maynard Hershon, are you?"

I confessed I was. She said she and her husband both read my articles and she'd bought my book and really liked the stories and how I wrote and all. I tried to listen and breathe silently as I pedaled 105 percent of comfortable, next to her on the hill.

I noticed I had to shout as we talked because she rode about half a bike-length ahead of me. A five-minute eternity passed as I continued chasing uphill just to stay even.

I thought about asking her if she recalled an article I wrote called "Half-Wheel Hell," about people who persist in riding next to you (sort of), their bottom bracket in line with your front axle. Surely she's read it, I thought.

I decided I wouldn't say anything, though. Funny. When this woman read that piece, she probably shook her head, remembering all the times some yo-yo half-wheeled her. She's getting even now, I thought.

Here's this woman, I imagined anaerobically, who says she's a fan of mine, says she's read my stuff for years. We're here on this hill, riding almost side by side. *Faithful a reader as she is,* you'd think she'd be a little curious about the person behind all those stories, the guy who wrote about the tight shorts, Volvos and the Cinelli in the cellar. But no...

Seems like she wants to drop the guy behind all those stories. Or she figures either she gets fit enough — today — for the Olympic Trials or she doesn't. It's two weeks after Thanksgiving, cold, and early in the ride, but let's stick a fork in the turkey from the back page of *VeloNews.* See if he's done.

I remembered that a week or so ago, my wife and I had gone to a Saturday night party. Eddie B, ex-U.S. national coach and the guy who wrote "Bicycle Road Racing," spoke briefly. Eddie told us that, in his years of coaching, he had to stay on top of European riders — many of whom were lazy trainers. U.S. guys, on the other hand, typically tended to overtrain. He'd had to watch them.

He told us he recommended taking it easy in the winter, getting some rest, doing alternative sports. Older riders, particularly, he said, should ease off drastically in winter months. Don't train hard, he said, train smart.

The next morning I rode with a dozen or so guys, mostly in their 30s and 40s, who had been at that party. Among us, *our* "celebrity guest," was the much-younger Ken Carpenter, the world-class match sprinter. You'd like Carpenter; I did. He's way too young and good-looking, maybe, too big across the shoulders, but a good guy nonetheless. Fun to talk with.

Carpenter, in this off-season, hadn't ridden his road bike for months; he'd been lifting weights and riding a mountain bike. Not a wiry roadie type, he hung in easily on the climb out of town, and for most of the 30-odd-mile ride. But he was dropped, yes I wrote dropped, by the lead group on the way home.

Yup. Ken Carpenter was visiting here, the guys had him out on a training ride and they dropped him on the way back to town.

But that wouldn't happen where you live. Your club would do it differently. You guys would ride with him and chat. You would never, never inhospitably drop him on your local roads just 'cause you felt momentarily frisky and he simply let you go. Would you? Sadly, maybe you would.

What would you show Ken Carpenter, dropping him like that? You'd show him you wanted to ride harder that day than he did. That a half-hour of December training—in a lifetime of riding — meant more to you than his company. That you so overflow with combative lust that (male or female) the odor of testosterone hovers around you.

Then, after the ride, you'd go home and take an Irish Spring shower and Ken Carpenter would go to the Olympic Games. You could watch on TV and root for him. You could remember the time he came on your club ride and you dropped him with about five miles to go. Guess you showed him, huh?

That's what I was thinking on that hill as I tried to keep pace with my woman fan who said she wasn't having a good day. Near the top of the hill, I asked her why I hadn't seen her out on club rides on weekends.

Oh, I'm not ready for those guys, she said, even though she had to know I ride with them most weeks and she evidently had no problem keeping up with me. No problem.

Her answer made me think of another story I'm sure she's read, one I wrote several years ago called "Miles." You might remember it. "Miles" is about a guy who trains like a triathlete possessed by demons, starves himself mountains-jersey-skinny, and thinks of nothing but cycling.

All the while he protests he isn't ready to race. Not yet. Not against "those guys." Those guys are way too serious, he says. Seriousness: sure is a lot of that stuff around. Check it out.

THE RIDERS

Again this year, I worked the Tour de Trump as photographer Darcy Kiefel's motor driver — as they say in bike-race parlance.

Darcy shoots the big races here and in Europe. She worked the Trump with a crew of three or four photographers, covering the road-race stages on motorcycles like mine. They'd arranged to sell photos to two U.S. monthly bike magazines, *BiciSport* (Italy) and *Sports Illustrated*.

Several of the shots in SI's Trump coverage were Darcy's, including the page-and-a-halfer next to the table of contents. I'm proud to write that she shot the photo of Trump winner Raúl Alcalá descending, right from the back seat of my motorcycle.

Each year at the Trump, the racers impress me all over again — as if I'd forgotten between events. It's not the speed so much, it's that — hey, *can those guys ride their bikes.*

For instance, I always watch them before races as they glide around the start areas: warming up; picking up and dropping off food and warmup clothing; chatting with support workers, fans and other riders; signing autographs; doing who knows what.

They pedal through crowds of fast-moving, preoccupied people, people busy doing important jobs of their own. The racers manage to ride around all those people, some of whom look like they're trying their hardest to get in the way. You witness a thousand miracles of bike control an hour.

The racers filter through the chaos, faces impassive, pedaling when they can, turning on nothing, standing motionless, whatever it takes. No problem.

When local cyclists — even classy, fit-looking ones — appear at starts or finishes on their bikes, you can tell immediately that they're spectators. Even if they wear PDM team jerseys, they don't look like PDM riders.

Most of us amateur bikie types don't resemble gazelles or greyhounds, it's true, but that's not why we're conspicuous in international-class company. We don't have that same fluid, effortless control, as if we were born on the bike. I know *I* don't. Sniff.

Those guys need that control, as you're probably aware. They often ride in fearful weather. They virtually and actually bump each other. They overlap handlebars, they touch wheels, they lean on each other in turns. They ride with one hand on the saddle of another bike, or on a car or motorcycle.

They eat on the bike, they pee while riding the bike, they get medical and mechanical attention on the bike.

When they get paced back up to the pack by a support car, they follow so close that their front wheel brushes the back bumper of the car. Bounces lightly off the bumper. Don't try that at home.

They do things that, if you or I did them, we'd simply crash. They do them regularly, just part of the job. After a while, I believe, they forget that all bike riders *can't* do them.

At one point, during a rainy road stage, Darcy asked me to stop in a driveway on a steep, twisty descent. She jumped off and ran across the road to set up on the inside of the corner and wait for the pack.

The guy whose driveway we'd invaded was standing in his yard, waiting for the race. He pointed at the off-camber, greasy-looking downhill bend in front of his house.

"This is the most dangerous corner on the hill," he warned us. "I get a bicycle a week, crashes here, maybe a motorcycle a month."

While I quickly jockeyed my motorcycle further off the road, out of the path of potential crashes, I thought about what he said. I decided I'd see how much trouble *these* bicycle riders had.

We stood side-by-side in the man's driveway, my shield up and dripping cold rain, as 130 bikes and riders swept over the brow of the hill and down on us, flowed around his corner and were gone.

That corner was, after all, one corner on one day in one race. Nothing memorable about it. No problem.

Darcy ran back across the road in a gap between a couple of team cars, grinned at us and hopped on the BMW, pulling on her helmet. We waved at the man standing there, slowly shaking his head in admiration. And then, we, too, were gone.

DEAR GREG

Dear Greg:

Way to go….

When we talked at the Giro, you smiled and said you didn't like racing at the back — just barely hanging on, trying not to get dropped in the mountains. You said your form was a long time coming.

I worried about you a little then. I thought, oh man, Greg seems kinda demoralized. Maybe he's not cut-out for riding "just okay," like some unknown in the bunch — adequate but unspectacular. No worries now, huh?

Thanks for telling me you had those misgivings, that you weren't seamlessly confident. I felt privileged, "in" somehow — in your confidence at least, not merely another journalist. You talked to me like a friend, a bike rider, not as someone there merely for an interview.

Because of that conversation in Italy, I know that on the trail back from your injuries and bad luck, you sometimes felt weak — maybe a little discouraged. Something about you — who knows what — kept you on the bike. Maybe the *same* something made you strong enough to ride 34 mph into Paris on Sunday.

Now, your perseverance has been rewarded by (what lots of people would call) a miracle. All over this country, presumably all over the world, bike riders and race fans are looking at each other, shaking their heads and saying, "unbelievable, unbelievable." And it *is* unbelievable, but it couldn't have happened to a nicer phenomenon.

Over the years, you've made it a pleasure every time we've met. When I see you in my mind's eye, you're smiling, saying, "hi, how're you — I read your stories."

That was enough for me, Greg. Just winning the '83 world's and being such a super guy was enough. Just winning the '86 Tour and being such a super guy; just going over there — American as apple pie and Greg Lemond — and beating guys we thought were unbeatable: those things were enough. And the whole time, being such a dependably, invariably super guy who loves to ride his bike. That was plenty. You were already a hero in my book; it was a done thing. You've been a hero of mine since the Avocet days, when you'd ride away from California's finest fields at Nevada City.

You didn't have to win the closest Tour in history to win me over. And you *certainly* didn't have to pull it out like you did, in the last seconds. You didn't have to win the Tour with shotgun pellets still in your heart; virtually no team left behind you; *nothing* behind you, in truth, but a couple of years of disappointing results.

Some guys gave up on you, Greg, after you lost 50 seconds, and with only that short time trial to get the time back. Guys said, "Well, he's done a hell of a ride anyway; only a couple of weeks ago, we didn't think he had much of a chance of finishing in the top 20." I never gave up. I thought, "Greg's done one impossible ride after another in this race. Maybe he'll do one more." I was afraid to tell people I still hoped, though, afraid I'd speak too soon and something awful would happen. But I never gave up.

I talk to guys at bike stores across the country in my job. Some of those guys wouldn't readily admit that it hurt to get thrown over their handlebars in a field sprint. But they told me they got choked-up watching you win that race. Said they could've cried. Some of 'em, Greg, *did* cry, I'll bet — maybe they'd tell you so if no one else could hear.

Race fans think about you coming back after nearly dying from the gunshot. They think about you coming back a little, and then needing surgery; then coming back yet again, and hurting your leg. They think about you barely being able to finish with the bunch in race after race, and still smiling — perhaps ironically, but smiling. Saying, hi, how're you doing.

They think about how many people wrote you off, claiming you didn't have it, didn't care any more, claiming you'd made such-and-such an amount of money and lost the hunger. Hey, he'd rather play golf.

When racing fans think about those things, and then sit riveted and watch while you take 58 seconds out of one of the strongest cyclists in the world; watch you pass your two-minute-man, the Tour favorite, Pedro Delgado; watch you walk away with the historic-best Tour de France in a cliff-hanging finale worthy of Indiana Jones; some of them get choked up, and maybe cry. You didn't have to do all that for *my* sake, Greg, you already had me.

We're all proud of you for beating Laurent Fignon, for snatching victory from him when he must have *known* he had it locked up. We're proud of you as an athlete, showman, and as a trier. He didn't lay down, we think, he didn't give up.

But Laurent Fignon is only, it seems to me, the *visible* opponent. The shotgun injury, the emergency surgery, the tendon problems, the slow recovery to form, *those* enemies, teamed-up to lead out the self-doubt that threatened you — and threatens us all, now and then. Self-doubt: the hardest guy to drop.

Thanks, Greg, for taking so much time out of that guy. Thanks for attacking at every opportunity, for hammering on the climbs and charging the descents, for putting your head down into Paris and shaking self-doubt — that cagey son-of-a-bitch — off your wheel.

Thanks, Greg, for showing us how it's done.

FELICE

I'm not telling you I spent most of today at Bianchi's *Reparto Corse* racing department simply to make you jealous. I'm not describing my lunch with Felice Gimondi, the last Italian to win the Tour ('65), to turn you celeste green with envy. These are things I do in my work. You talk about *your* job, don't you?

I've been a Gimondi fan as long as I've been riding. My first racing bike was a Bianchi just like Gimondi rode his entire career, except for a year-or-so on Bianchi-owned Chiordas. He and I are about the same age, size and build and I always thought we looked a little alike. *I* like to think so, anyway.

Because Gimondi's and Eddy Merckx's racing careers spanned virtually the same period, the Italian star's opportunities were "cannibalized." Even riding in that famous shadow, Gimondi did well enough to rank with countrymen Coppi, Bartali and Moser as super-champions.

I saw him twice last year, at the Giro and at a trade show, where he represented Bianchi. I thought he seemed stiff, maybe a little humorless, but now I realize it was the circumstances. Watch him among people he knows, among Bianchi people, among Italians. He speaks quietly, and moves in what I'd call a graceful way. He's relaxed, genial and interested in other folks' ideas.

He's got that gentle style, if you know what I mean. You watch him walk around the Bianchi plant. Everyone's glad to see him; they're smiling, exchanging greetings. They like each other.

Gimondi led our party on a factory tour, assisted by two interpreters. Right away, we noticed a poster on the *Reparto Corse* wall showing Gimondi and two other Bianchi people standing around a team car. In the picture, Gimondi's face has a big "X" drawn across it.

One of us asked about the X; Gimondi and the mechanic standing with him laughed. Someone had X'd him out because he had a reputation, he said: He used to tell people to go away before races, wanting to be left alone. "I was always a nervous racer," he told me. "No, not really?," I responded, genuinely surprised. "Oh, really," he said, "always."

I guess he's gained 15 or 20 pounds since he quit racing, but he carries it well. He says he mostly rides a mountain bike these days. He likes to get away from the traffic, out to the country where it's quiet. He grins and says the style of the mountain bike better suits his age — late 40s, I believe. His face is lined from the sun, but he's still slender and fit-looking. I remember thinking it'd be fun to go riding with him, to see if I could stay on his wheel, maybe. He's too nice to hurt me, I figured.

As you watch, you can see that the other workers at Bianchi — guys with torches, guys with brooms, guys with ties on — all love Gimondi. Everybody's smiling, as if they're glad to be there.

The truth is, Italians generally seem happy in their jobs. People appeared enthusiastic not only about their own products, but about sport generally. Every factory we visited had walls plastered with autographed posters, photos, framed jerseys and old metal signs. Their walls look just like you wish your garage walls could.

They're cycling crazy there, in a civilized way. No one came to work at Bianchi that Monday morning, unaware of who'd just won the "*Giro de Francia*." Trust me: they knew.

In the *Reparto Corse*, we watched as workmen cut and machine-mitered tubing; brazed and filed frames and forks; and checked them on the same kind of electronic-readout, flat table I saw last year at Moser. A worker grabbed a frame off a hook and rechecked it for us — it read so straight you'd get bored counting decimal places.

We saw lots of Shimano components on mountain and road bikes at Bianchi. As we stood around a Columbus MAX pro-bike, squeezing the brake levers, we asked Gimondi — half-teasing — if he were outfitting a team today, would he choose traditional Italian or Shimano equipment. He dodged that one deftly, explaining with a grin that choosing team equipment is never as simple as it might seem. It's always a political decision, he said. I guess when you're a monument yourself, you're not free to speak evil of other monuments.

The last Italian to have won the Tour sat across the table from me in the Bianchi lunchroom. We shared a bottle of *acqua minerale*. Sometimes I poured; sometimes he did. I felt, between you and me, that I was just where I was supposed to be.

Gimondi and the Bianchi guys asked us about trends in the U.S., about road and mountain bikes. We talked about what we liked personally, and what we thought the market demanded.

We talked, through the interpreter, about Greg LeMond, who had just defeated Claudio Chiappucci in France. I said I thought Chiappucci's effort had been magnificent, heroic. We asked Gimondi what he thought about the LeMond-inspired revolution in pro salaries. He grinned and said he was only sorry he'd raced at the wrong time.

I must have asked him some giveaway questions, because Gimondi nodded his head across the table at me at one point, and asked our interpreter, "a cyclist, this one, no?"

I sat there across from my first hero in cycling, Felice Gimondi, and I smiled. Wouldn't you? Picked as a fellow cyclist by your own idol. Hey, I admit it; I was thrilled.

A cyclist? Oh, yes.

WHO WON?

Years ago, I worked in a Honda motorcycle store. I got to know a guy who called on us, selling us parts and accessories. He used to point out that some of his competitors, other reps, weren't motorcyclists at all.

"They don't even ride," he'd say. "They don't care about motorcycles. They're not enthusiasts. They're only going to be working in the industry for a few years, siphoning income away from those of us who *do* care, who *do* ride, who'll be around the industry for life."

That's what he'd say. Somehow, though, I knew the situation wasn't that simple, I kind of agreed. I thought then that people working in enthusiast businesses should be enthusiasts, and I still think so.

So let's agree that a person who works around motorcycles ought to ride motorcycles. But think how much *more* important participation is in cycling — a lifestyle sport — a sport that must be practiced with regularity and discipline.

You can ride your motorcycle on occasional sunny Sundays; if your battery hasn't gone dead you'll do fine. Try that on your 10-speed and you will *not* have fun.

I hadn't thought about my old rep for years, but I was reminded of his words today — the Monday after Greg LeMond's icing-on-the-cake victory at the 1989 World Championships. While doing my job selling parts to bike shops by phone, I always mentioned the news about Greg's success. Many shop employees had already heard how Greg outsprinted Sean Kelly. They knew about how few racers had finished the rainy, hilly world's. They'd read the papers and learned about how the other famous names had done.

But plenty of shop people had no idea there'd been a world's that Sunday. No one at those shops saw the TV reports or read the papers. No one got called by an excited friend with the news of Greg's victory. No one at those shops knew Greg had become only the fifth man ever to win the Tour and the world's the same year, even though all that stuff was reported on the radio and in Monday's sports pages — big news — even for non-cycling fans.

I felt surprised and dismayed. I couldn't believe that my mention of Greg's gritty win could've surprised employees in so many stores, and I thought about my old rep's words about enthusiasts in enthusiast businesses.

I asked myself if I would send a friend who had gotten interested in performance cycling, who needed help from a pro-style shop, to a store where no one knew Greg LeMond won the world's. Do golf shop employees who care about golf know, the next morning, who won the U.S. Open? Do tennis store workers follow world-class tennis? Gee, I *think* so.

Does it make any difference if your shop cares about bicycle racing at the highest level? Will your new bike be better assembled, your new wheels truer, your tune-up sharper? Probably not.

Maybe you're a recreational rider, a century rider or a tourist, and your ambition is to cross Iowa or Australia on your bike. Maybe you're a triathlete and you'd simply like to get set up on a bike that fits well and doesn't cost you time. Maybe you're a mountain biker and enjoy getting off by yourself or blasting down trails with the guys. If you're one of those people, your shop knowing about Greg at the world's won't matter, is my thought.

But maybe you like the idea of riding in a pack of bikies, in a "chain gang," as they say in England. Maybe you'd enjoy learning how to fold a sew-up spare the way bikies do, worldwide. Maybe you'd like to road race someday. Or maybe hearing or reading names like Coppi, Merckx and LeMond runs chills up and down your permanently curved, sweaty spine. Maybe you'd cut a ride short to get home in time for Tour de France TV coverage. Maybe you wish you knew Italian so you could read *Bicisport* articles about your favorite European star.

If you do wish you spoke Italian or French, if you intend to ride all the passes of the Tour de France: Stop by your bike store the morning after something *you* think is significant happens in cycling. Something you truly care about. If nobody there knows and nobody there cares, do the right thing.

TOUR DE WASTELAND

Yes, I watched the 1992 Olympic Women's Road Race last night. And yes, I agree: The coverage was the pits, the worst I've ever seen, especially after three luxurious weeks of ESPN's French-footage Tour stuff.

Yep, I heard the announcer tell the world about the quarter-inch wide tires on the bicycles. I realize no one mentioned the name of the third U.S. woman, who eventually placed 10th. Not once. Hey, if I were Sally Zack — dude, I'd be miffed. She's nicer than me, though....

We learned the breeding history of Inga Thompson's horse. We learned the length of Inga's braid. But we never learned why she fell off her bike during the women's Olympic road race. We didn't get to see that.

We saw and heard how everyone hates Jeannie Longo. She gets snapped at by her own dog, we suppose. We were told how much she loves to win. We learned how the entire pack watches her, ready to counter her every vicious move. We know all that; we *don't* know how the hell she got away alone to chase Kathryn Watt. We missed that part, too.

Waiting in vain to find out how Thompson fell or how Longo got away, we quietly sat through more than two hours of unbearably tedious (to me at least), world-class diving and gymnastics. We absorbed, without protest, what felt like a couple of hundred commercial messages.

Over and over, lanky Randy Travis opined about how folks around the world — all alike under their variously colored skins — just love to share frosty Cokes. In contrast, during the short interludes between "one-world" Coke ads, "wild-man" medal-winners spouted unscripted, embarrassing America-*uber-alles* crap. That stuff is inevitable, I figure, every four years. All that chauvinism could've been saved for the Republican convention....

What an indictment, I thought. TV is truly a wasteland. I vowed, as I watched audacious Kathryn Watt's solo finish, that that was the last moment of Olympic coverage I'd be suckered into watching. And it will be.

Most nights of the year you can forget that TV-program material is merely bait; it lures you into a seated position in front of the ads. Bait. Even Murphy Brown. Even the first season of "Wiseguy." Even "Law and Order," even "Seinfeld" (No! Yes). Most nights you can forget. No way could you forget for more than a moment last night.

The women's Olympic road race ... right. Any Olympics now, the network'll break just after the field sprint starts, 200 meters from the finish. They'll run five or six ads, then let you watch the first few riders cross the line. Then, as handlers wipe the exhausted winner's face, credits will scroll over the picture. The voice-over will tell you how white your shirts can be.

Outfits like Coke paid big money for air time during Games' broadcasts, knowing we'd be glued to our screens. And we *were*, weren't we? Darned right. How could any American fail to respond to symbols of U.S. pride like the official snack food or 4-wheel drive minivan of the umpteenth Olympic Games?

As you watched, you got the idea that somebody paid way more money for — and way more attention to — the Coke ad than the road race. The one-minute Coke ad was perfect, no detail amiss. No camera angle, no nuance, was ignored. We learned every goldarn thing we need to know about Coke and its global popularity. Hurray. The Coke ad kicked butt, took names.

Ah, but we turned on the TV to watch the Olympic road race. And, gosh, we didn't learn very much about *that*. But hey, how much does the race matter, really? Someone wins, someone loses; in four years they'll have another one. New heroes, new villains. Inga, schminga.

The Coke ad, now, the Coke ad matters. The Coke ad will make a difference where it counts, where it rustles and clinks and trickles on down — in the pay envelopes and cash registers of America. When Coke wins, we win. America wins.

Inga missed the break, but Coke, read my lips, Coke kicked butt for America. Makes you proud, don't it? Does me.

OCH'

Before I worked the Tour DuPont as a motorcycle driver, I'd had the wrong idea about what it was like to drive in race caravans. I guess I thought all those cars and motorcycles traveled at race pace, maybe 18 to 25 mph. I imagined support drivers yawning, hoping a rider would raise an arm for help, just for something to do.

I was wrong. Sure, at times the pace is slow and boring. Other times — times that stick in one's memory — the pace gets crazy and the driving frenzied, virtually hostile. You learn to ride with one eye watching the road ahead and the other obsessively scanning your mirrors. Have to, to survive.

After each stage, we motorcycle drivers gather in our hotel bar to watch the ESPN coverage of the day's racing. We look at each other, knowing that the things we'd done that day are impossible in the real world. You can only do them in a race caravan — and then only with luck.

To give you a clearer picture of the caravan action, here's a brief primer: A commissaire's car follows the pack; the motorcycle drivers wait behind that car for clearance to ride up through the pack or the break. We wait right in front of the line of team cars, between them and the riders they serve: a place where no one with good sense wants to be.

Team drivers loathe any impediment to their instant passage up to a raised-hand rider. We moto-folks can be impediments, but we're easily dealt with. They have big vehicles; we have little ones. They intimidate us out of the way with reckless, horn-honking, foot-to-the-floor aggressiveness.

The thought of such aggressiveness brings to mind Jim Ochowicz of the Motorola Professional Cycling Team (previously, of course, 7-Eleven).

Och' drives hard. All the support people know he does. But they agree he drives well and has not killed anyone that anyone can remember. The Motorola team boss drives European-caravan style: he asks no quarter and gives none.

Any space Och' leaves you on any side of his Volvo team car is enough space, luxurious, spread-your-wings kinda space. If he forgets he has bicycles mounted on quick-release racks on each side, sticking out from the sides of the car, well, hey, he's got a lot to think about, his riders doing so well and all.

I knew before my first tour that Och' drove that way. Still, I was unprepared for the intensity we experienced.

I remember chief race photographer Darcy Kiefel and me following the pack, as fast as I could wrestle my BMW through a downhill series of curves marked 15 mph, dirty slimy-looking water streaming across the apexes.

Foolishly, I glanced at one of my mirrors, taking a huge chance looking away from the road during that intensely dangerous moment. My mirror was full of Pontiac grill. Pontiac: they build excitement.

It was Och', drifting the corners in his then Pontiac station wagon, 18 inches from my license plate. I was wide open, tapped out for nerve, tossing that big motorcycle, with its fairing, stuffed saddlebags, 15 pounds of junk and telephoto lenses in the tank bag, me and Darcy on board.

We can't go on meeting like this, I said to myself, trying to maintain bowel control.

So that night — digestion calm but blood pressure still high — I complained about Och' at a caravan meeting. My whining met with mixed response. Some people said they felt Och' knew what he was doing. Others recalled horrific incidents of their own. An official promised he'd speak to Och', but people in the know doubted he would ease off. That's Och', they said.

Don't tell him you're scared, they advised. He'll just get worse.

My friend Bruce Gottlieb came over, told me he'd admired my courage in speaking up about Och's driving. Bruce drove one of the medical motors, carrying a race doctor. Usually, Bruce and his passenger would ride right behind the commissaire's car.

Because the 7-Eleven team led that tour virtually from the start, Och' held front position in the line of team cars, right behind Bruce. Bruce said early in the race he'd had several terrifyingly close encounters.

But after a few days, maybe after our caravan meeting, Bruce told me he noticed Och' driving in a more civilized manner. Not cautiously, not Och', but leaving a little room for comfort.

So Bruce approached Och' after a stage and told him that for a while he'd had Och' pegged as a total a—h—e, but now he thought Och' might be okay. Och' grinned.

From then on, Bruce tried to take care of Och' when he could. If he saw the 7-Eleven Pontiac returning from a visit to the pack, he'd drop back and open a hole for the team manager. Then Bruce would accelerate, and Och' would drop back in behind him.

They didn't ever discuss that proceedure; Bruce just did it. I guess it seemed like the thing to do.

Well, 7-Eleven's Dag-Otto Lauritzen won the race and his team took the team prize. After the award ceremony, Och' found Bruce in the Atlantic City Boardwalk finishing-area crowd, and gave him two team hats, signed by all the victorious 7-Eleven racers.

The next morning, Bruce loaded his motorcycle on a truck for shipment back to Colorado, said so long to his bike-race friends and flew home to Boulder. It's been weeks since I've seen him … but I have a hunch ol' Bruce is still smiling.

WHAT SEATS!

Another Tour DuPont, 1993, in the books. Again, I "drove" one of Mavic's two neutral tech-support motors. If you watched on ESPN, that was my mechanic-passenger Greg Miller, holding spare wheels in the air, behind Van Itterbeeck at Winston-Salem; and doing the wheel-change with Alcalá on the bridge in Richmond.

This race came off well, I thought, with none of the glitches we suffered in the first couple of (Trump) years. Each year it gets smoother. No awful crashes on wet, steel-grate bridges; no confusing, impossible-to-marshal Atlantic City time trial courses.

But there were developments that made some people nervous. Dave "Lumpy" Williams didn't return as race director this year, and the race entered (beautiful) North Carolina for the first time.

But, far as I could see, Lumpy's replacement — my hero, David Mayer-Oakes, from Lubbock, Texas — filled Lumpy's sizeable shoes in fine style. And North Carolina's participation was as competent and enthusiastic as anyone could wish for.

Schools closed for the race, particularly through Virginia and North Carolina. Thousands of kids of all ages and their teachers lined the roads; waving, holding signs ("Go USA"; "Where's Greg?"), staring open-mouthed at the spectacle (especially in sprint towns), and grinning and waving at us support people.

In towns, businesses emptied so workers could watch the race go by. In the country, folks drove cars or tractors to the ends of their driveways and sat there to watch. Men with old hot-rods or Corvettes or bicycle collections brought them out so we could admire them as we passed.

I met an old hero, Jan Raas, from the old Peter Post-Raleigh days. Raas, a modest, quiet-spoken guy, drove the WordPerfect team van, and only tried to kill me with it once or twice. I saw Dickie Dunn from the old CRC of A-Raleigh days. Dunn had come over from Asheville, in western North Carolina, for the last day or so of the race. Unlike Raas, Dickie didn't try to kill me even once.

And the riders.... I remember cresting a hill somewhere and starting down the descent, grateful that the road was wide and not so curvy that I'd have problems staying out of the riders' way.

As we got to speed, a racer in front of me went to the left road edge; took his left foot out of the pedal; twisted his body on the bike; put the foot up somewhere around his rear brake; dug out his whatchacallit and began peeing — at maybe 45 mph. In a sweeping curve. (The road, not the stream.)

Here's a Steve Hegg story. I know I tell one every year after the DuPont, but I always see him doing something memorable. Hegg was in the front 15 or 20 on Beech Mountain — 10 uphill miles, some steep, some super steep. At that point, 80 or 90 great riders were behind him, struggling on the climb.

Miller and I were floating toward the front on the motor, supporting riders whose team vehicles were trapped way back behind the slower climbers. Hegg (Chevrolet-LA Sheriff) and Miller — I should mention — are buddies from Southern California.

A mile or so from the top, Hegg rides over to us, his sunglasses in his hand, and says to Miller: "Greg, would you take these to the top for me, if it wouldn't be too much trouble?"

Miller says "Sure, Steve," pockets the sunglasses, and off we go up the road. Miller shakes his head. "That Steve...." he says, and explains that Hegg could easily have put the glasses in a jersey pocket. But Hegg likes to make Miller feel involved, that he's helping Hegg somehow. Like carrying his glasses to the top of the hill.

So next time you feel yourself about to lose your cool after an undistinguished finish at the grueling, 40-mile Pleasantville road race — perhaps about to yell at someone who in no way deserves your anger — remember Steve Hegg, whose cool never deserts him. Hegg is considerate even when no one expects any consideration at all.

Miller and I followed Alcalá, Armstrong and Kvalsvoll up the last part of the Beech Mountain climb. There were the two of us, a TV motor, an official named John Asaro — riding solo on his motorcycle and making sure no press or TV vehicles interfered in the bike race — and, of course, Raúl, Lance and Atle.

Lance jumped three times. The abrupt power of his attacks took my breath away. Those guys had already ridden 150 hilly miles and they'd been climbing for the last 10. Atle and Raul, it seemed to me, were content to set a steady pace. Not Lance.

My speedometer read 12 or 13 mph, maybe 15. You'd watch Lance: When one pedal went down, he'd be going 15; when the other went down, he'd be going 25. Now. Instantly. Pure sudden power on that steep slope after all those leg-breaking miles and vertical feet.

Eventually, Raúl could chase him down. He could do it once, then twice, but he couldn't do it the third time. Maybe it was a costly few GC seconds gained for Lance, but — oh my — it was something to see. You could get an idea on TV but I wish you could've been there with us. You won't see "hit" like that often, I promise.

As we watched, black-and-white-striped stern-guy official Asaro — momentarily free of policing duties — drifted over to us and caught my eye. Asaro grinned. "What seats," he said.

What seats is right. What a race. Wish you could've been there.

SARA

Sara Neil, from Vancouver, has ridden Olympic road races and been Canadian national champ in three events. Neil is tall, and built strong but sleek. She looks you in the eye and says what she's thinking.

Schoolteacher Neil, clearly, can ride. On the bike, she has that textbook flat back, relaxed, long-legged, real-rider look. Pushes biggish gears. She's tough as nails. As a Power Bar wrapper.

But kind. Neil, 31, worked as an instructor at an Alex Stieda Training Camp I attended in Whistler, B.C., in August. At camp, Neil helped me with things like cornering, things I've always done in certain intuitive ways. Stieda and Neil do those things differently — about twice as fast.

New ways come slowly to me. Neil looked out for me and gave me minimum heat. You can tell she loves to hand it out and take it, too, but she mostly treated me gently.

Last fall, Neil's docs found a grapefruit-size cyst on an ovary. It scared her, I think, but you'd have to have known her a while before she'd admit it. Docs cut the cyst out, but she went through months of chemotherapy making sure the awfulness was gone.

The treatments made her weak and sick; most of her hair fell out. She rode an indoor trainer to keep active. She lost virtually all her fitness anyway.

Now, Neil's hair's grown in; she's been back on her bike for months. She's plenty fit. I didn't realize *how* fit till the camp's last day.

We did three hours out of Whistler on a rolling highway. We jammed down the road in a steady tail wind, about 10 of us roadie campers, two abreast on the wide shoulder. We sailed up the hills and hit 50 mph down 'em. Neil sat at, or near, the front. Looked strong.

I sat in, working as little as possible on my borrowed, ultra-light racing bicycle. Did pretty well, considering the pace and the 90-degree heat. I felt good: warm, loose, the beginnings of confidence. Tail wind....

An hour-and-a-half out we turned around, Neil still at the front, strong-looking as ever. Me? The wind wanted me stopped dead in the highway. I climbed fast as I could, sweating, slipping behind on the grades. Working so hard I forgot to drink.

At the bottom of one of the hills, Stieda suggested we have some fun. Right. He divided us into pairs, an instructor and a camper, and partnered me with Sara Neil. First team to the top wins, he said.

Instructor Bob Roll grabbed his partner's arm and began to drag him up the grade. I sat behind Neil, determined not to get left behind. She dropped back and pushed me by the seat of my shorts, then grabbed the back of my jersey and yanked me up the hill. I tried my hardest, suffering like a hell-bound sinner.

She'd push me a while, then drag me, then I'd try to draft behind her. She began slinging me up the hill. I'd try to maintain the momentum long as I could. I hurt.

Somehow, she heaved me at the precise right second. I pedaled around the lead guys and crested that hill in front. We'd won. I'd have loved to have gotten off my bike to celebrate, but we still had 10 miles to ride.

The pace hardly slowed. I hung until my calves reacted to my dehydration and began to cramp. I climbed into the follow van, listened to tapes and watched flat-backed Sara Neil hammer at the front. Slow enough so campers could hang, fast enough so everyone was working.

I don't often ride that hard. I can't remember the last time I didn't finish a road ride. Maybe you'd have thought it was easy — maybe not.

And Sara Neil? Neil finished fresh, thank you. Did I mention that Neil rode her mountain bike that afternoon? On 2.125-inch-big, fat, road-howlin' knobby tires. Whatta woman.

How does she do that? It ain't trick bike parts or magic food. It's class. She's gifted physically, she works her ass off, she rests, she's always learning. Give her my regards if you run into her on a B.C. vacation. Nice Canadian girl. Tell her I said that.

LIFESTYLES OF THE FAST & FAMOUS

Used to be at trade shows, I'd want something — a bike or a jersey or some outrageous paint job. I don't lust for bike stuff any more but I do love seeing the people at the shows and hearing the stories.

Here are a couple of stories I heard at Interbike '91, held in Anaheim in September.

Greg LeMond almost never comes to trade shows, but his presence is always there. You see his picture, sometimes five times life size, endorsing this or that product. People talk about him, about how only Greg's endorsement generates impact outside the pure enthusiast market. While all this conversation and commerce swirls around his image, Greg the man is somewhere far away.

I saw Bob LeMond, Greg's dad, in the hotel lobby one morning. I told him my friends and I thought that, athletics aside, he'd raised a hell of a fine boy, that Greg had been unfailingly nice to me and to people he didn't know from a load of hay.

Bob said he thought Greg was pretty okay, too. We got to chatting; Bob told me that when Greg calls home from Europe, he has to ask his son about what happened in the race that day or that weekend. Greg won't bring it up unless Bob asks.

If Bob does ask, Greg will tell him how he did, bare bones, never describing how the race went, never: "I missed the one break but it got reeled in and I got in the second one, and we stayed away for..." He never supplies the details. Usually wants to talk about fishing, Bob said. Loves fly fishing.

Bob said, "Greg was on a fishing trip after the world's and caught a fairly sizable, small-mouth bass. He was about to throw it back but stopped himself, thinking he'd show it to his fishing buddy back at the lodge.

"When he walked in with the fish, the guides grabbed it, weighed and measured it, examined the rod and line he'd used, photographed everything and took statements from Greg and Kathy about the catch.

"Turned out it was the largest small-mouth bass caught on that particular rod and line — ever. Greg's name went into the record book. He's now a world champion bass fisherman...."

Eddy Merckx *was* at the show and stories about him circulate like mad. Somehow, even though industry people see him often, and his riding days seem more distant every year, he still has that aura ... that strength ... that ... well, you know.

And speaking of Merckx, Chuck Schmidt introduced himself to me at the show. Schmidt, some years ago, designed the Eddy Merckx logo — not the EM bicycle you see on head tubes, but the stylized name that makes you think of Merckx bikes (go ahead, try not to). The logo that, in decal form, may lean against your room wall as you read this. Schmidt told me two stories about Eddy.

Schmidt said he designed the logo and received a bike as payment. Rode the bike, loved it. Meanwhile, the image Schmidt created became Merckx's. When you visit the factory, you'll see that familiar 10-letter icon over the entrance.

Sometime later, Schmidt, who'd kept in occasional touch with his client and cycling hero, got a call from Merckx.

"I'm really happy with the logo," Merckx said, "I've had lots of satisfaction from it. I'd like to give you another bike. Tell me what tubing you'd like, dimensions, equipment and color. I'll build it right away."

Schmidt did just as Merckx told him, unwilling to argue with The Cannibal. He's now riding a red-fade-to-white 753 Merckx. Schmidt says people regularly ask him about the bike, which, of course, he loves, and he's happy to answer questions — except one.

"When people ask me where I got it," he says, "I don't know what to say. Doesn't feel right, me telling 'em Eddy himself gave it to me."

Schmidt said that during the selection process, Merckx visited him at home to look at logo designs. The two men sat at a wooden table on a large deck behind the house. Schmidt had brought out a book, a coffee-table-sized guide to cycling from the mid-'70s. In addition to explaining how derailleurs work, the book presented photos from cycling history. One photo, a double-page spread, had been shot from above, maybe from a hillside, during a Tour de France mountain stage.

It showed the pack at the base of a mountain. In the distance, you could see snow-capped peaks. Nearer, you could see the road climbing, winding in an endless series of switchback turns up the mountain. You saw the riders bunched together in shared dread of the painful ascent.

You saw Merckx, in yellow (Faema team), already six or eight bike lengths in front of the pack, already attacking at the very bottom of the climb.

Schmidt, who had marked the page with a rainbow ribbon unstitched from a worn-out cycling cap, opened the book to the photo and put it in front of Merckx. Eddy looked at it for a good long time, shook his head slightly, side to side. And said very quietly, "Boy, that was fun."

SMILIN' GEORGE

Last night, George Mount came home. And at a Berkeley Bike Club meeting, Mount — '70s Euro-pro, Red Zinger winner, pro world's competitor — talked about race tactics and told stories about the old days. He told us how he started in racing, "dumb as they come."

"Now," he said, "I work all the time. I'm out of shape and 20 pounds overweight; I only ride criteriums. I like guys who are just like I was then — dumb, strong, work-ethic guys who have to take hard pulls or they feel guilty. Now, I pull through a couple of times, no more.

"I sit seven to 12 riders back, in what I call the 'sweet spot,'" he said, "off to the side so I don't get boxed in. That way if something happens that looks good I can go with it. If I drift back in the pack, I look for someone else who's going up and sit on their wheel — they take me up. I try never to do the work myself until the end.

"You can be 20 times stronger than me, but if there are no hills you'll never drop me. I let you do all the work you want to, then I beat you at the end. I'm riding on experience, grit and ego."

Mount said racers in the U.S. didn't — and still don't — know how to ride in crosswinds, in echelons. "Guys here don't have a clue. If you can't ride echelons in Europe, you might as well pack up your stuff."

Someone asked Mount why people called him "Smilin' George." "I'd get in a two-up break," he explained. "The two of us would hammer for all we were worth. Then, when I felt about as bad as I could feel, and I figured the other guy did, too, I'd look over at him and grin.

"That would often give the guy motivational problems."

He reminded us of the story about two guys away together on a brutally hot day. Both run out of water. One guy fakes it: Every quarter mile or so, he takes his bottle out of the cage and pretends to drink. The other guy watches, getting thirstier and thirstier. Soon he sits up and quits pedaling, done for the day.

He said when he got to Italy, the coaches told him cycling is 80 percent mental, and only 20 percent heart, lungs and legs. He said you had to *allow* yourself to win. And you had to *need* to win; you had to be hungry. "Too hard, otherwise," George said.

He told us he thinks preparation is more important, perhaps, than tactics. He said he always put his bag of gear together the night before the race. Not only did he not arrive at events without his shoes or shorts, many times he brought *two* pairs. "Kinda anal," was the phrase he used.

He said he'd walk courses before events. Sometimes he'd touch the road surface in the corners with his hand, testing for traction. He wanted to know everything he could about the course, for times when he might need to change line suddenly, or attack just before a corner.

Mount said he always tried to have a plan, an idea of how the race might develop. Most times, though, he said, shaking his head, the race would refuse to go according to his scheme.

He said he thought the best time to attack was just after a break was caught and absorbed. The pack would relax a moment, you could jump up the road, and sometimes no one would chase. Riders would look at each other, waiting for the other guy to go first.

Mount said that he liked riding with only one teammate, and that Mark Pringle was his favorite. Near the ends of criteriums, Mark, a time trialist type, would accelerate off the front of the group as hard as he could, his partner in tow. "Then the second guy, the better sprinter, would come around, like the second stage of a missile. The booster would drop back and block. We won lots of races that way."

Mount talked about trying to support himself in the '70s, racing in the West — surely below poverty level — then getting a stipend of $100-a-month and thinking that was pretty good money.

He said he didn't race much in the East because he didn't have a car to drive there. Nor enough money to get there any other way. He had worked at Velo-Sport — the shop where the meeting was held — and had lived upstairs (free), the guest of Peter Rich, the owner.

He talked about arriving to race in Europe and realizing that he didn't know who the danger men were. And because he didn't know a European language, he couldn't learn anything listening to conversations in the pack.

"You have to know the other riders," he said. "Combinations are the key in breakaways. Watch riders you know are strong. Check who attacks. One strong guy from each of the good teams is perfect. Go with them, or look for someone strong to tow you up to them before they get too far up the road. Their team-mates will shut the pack down or slow it enough to make the break work."

Eventually, Mount joined an Italian pro team, Sammontana. His teammates noticed him reading a book, a popular science-fiction novel he had bought at the airport. Noting the lack of pictures in the book, they began to regard Mount as the team intellectual.

"A comic book would last them eight stages," Mount said.

On Sammontana, Mount rode exactly the same size bike as team leader Roberto Visentini. So, Smilin' George's job was to stay with Visentini, at least until the last climb, in case Smilin' Roberto needed a quick bike-change.

Someone asked Mount to "tell some race stories." Mount said it was difficult for him to remember individual races.

"I've ridden thousands of them," he said.

He told us that one season, right after the Giro, he realized that during the previous 50 days, he'd raced all but five.

"It was eat, sleep and ride your bike," he said, "but no drugs. You don't need drugs to race the bike."

He smiled into his notes.

"Besides," he quipped, "drugs were for recreation."

STANDING THE HEAT

I worked the '89 Tour de Trump as Darcy Kiefel's motorcycle driver. Darcy's job was chief staff photographer for the tour.

We rode a BMW R100RS to put Darcy where she wanted to be to get good shots. We press-photo people get to ride in front of, behind, and through the race, so we see what happens as well as anyone.

The above two paragraphs might sound matter-of-fact, as if I were used to seeing Trump-style racing. Truth to tell, I feel anything but matter-of-fact. Working the Tour de Trump was a fantasy journey in BikeRaceLand, 10 days with the circus.

Finally, almost unbelievably, we have U.S. bike racing as we've always wanted it to be. Working in the caravan at that first event was the most intense, gratifying trip imaginable.

I'd like to tell you everything, but memories pile up on top of one another. I *will* tell you about a hill on the first road stage, from Albany to New Paltz, New York. Maybe that'll give you some idea....

The race bible listed Devil's Kitchen as a difficult hill and warned us about possible mud slides. Some of the teams, the smart and lucky ones, put on big freewheel cogs, 23s and 24s. Their riders could pedal up the hill. Guys with 21s did not fare so well.

But Darcy and I didn't need low gear — we had 1000cc of motorcycle to get us up the hill. Neither of us was familiar with eastern terrain. Neither had been to upstate New York until the tour. Up to that point, since the Albany start, the hills hadn't been too bad.

We asked each other, how bad could this one be? We decided we'd go up with the front group.

When I saw the hill my heart went to my mouth. I later heard it described as 17 percent to 20 percent, but who knows? It was super-steep and narrow; a rough, old, broken-up road. Water an inch or so deep streamed down the hill; you couldn't see the road surface. You could only see the shiny surface of the water. Mudslides covered the road in places. The shoulders were soft mud; your foot sank right in.

You couldn't see any other motorcycles; just Darcy and me, with the bicycles — ridden by the best in the world — on that awful hill. The riders in front, the ones you saw on TV, did fine. With some momentum and a clear road, they could sit in their saddles and pedal right up the hill.

Other riders, with high gears or without luck, got balked on the hill and had to slow down or outright stop. Lots of those guys — and the two of us on the motor — ended up stalled on the climb.

The motorcycle felt huge as a motorhome on that one-lane hill. Even though I steered over until the wheels sat half on the pavement, half on the mud shoulder, it took up way too much room. I had to be careful not to put my (and Darcy's, and the motorcycle's) weight on my outside foot. If that foot sank in the mud, we'd slowly tip over, down the shoulder into muddy trouble.

Meanwhile, dozens of bike riders, some of the best bike riders in the world, walked and yelled for pushes and zig-zagged up the hill, crisscrossing the road in front of us like novices, stopping our progress. So many riders clogged the road I couldn't keep the BMW moving forward. The engine protested, faltered, trying to die.

The scene got more and more unreal — I realized we didn't dare stop and we sure couldn't go. Whatever we did, we were totally *in the way*....

Then we crossed paths with a rider going from side to side in the road in front of us. We stopped just in time, clumsily. He fell over into us, crying, swearing almost incoherently at us in what sounded like English, but, as many times as I've tried to remember, I'm not sure.

I recall him being tall and skinny. I remember his jersey was busy with printing, but if he were sitting across the table from me at dinner, I wouldn't know him as the racer who fell into us.

I caught him as he toppled over onto my leg. I helped him back onto his feet and wheels, all the while trying to hold the motorcycle up.

He couldn't get started again on that streaming wet steep hill without a push. He kept wailing, a stream of syllables that occasionally sounded like words, calling for someone to push him. But help was not forthcoming; other guys had their problems, too.

Darcy, who'd climbed off the motorcycle to shoot pictures on the hill, (when in hot water, take a bath), jumped back on. I got the Beemer going again, and tried to find a way up through the craziness, up and away to someplace where I could forget I'd ever heard that people race bicycles.

I heard guys yelling, "Hey, get that goddam motorcycle out of here". I could smell clutches burning, smell hot engines. Two motorcycles needed work — serious work — I heard later, after the Devil's Kitchen climb. Rental vans got old in two miles.

I stalled the engine twice trying to keep from hitting riders crossing in front of us. Two guys on another motorcycle close behind, trying to follow us up the hill, barely got stopped in time to avoid hitting us. Sorry, guys, I said, though no one could hear. Sorry.

I got Darcy and me to the top and we got out of the riders' way for the descent. My undershirt lay cold, soaked, against my back.

I thought: Well, Maynard, you dreamed of driving a press motor in a European-style race and here you are. How do you like it?

I thought about how I'd felt I'd interfered with the race, gotten in the way. Then I thought: Hey, if Darcy and I hadn't been there, doing our job the best we could, who would shoot the pictures? Who would come home and sit down and type this story?

Who would tell you fans what happened on Devil's Kitchen at the real Tour de Trump, where TV can hardly go?

Still, I couldn't get settled in my mind about it. I worried it around in my head like a dog with a bone, wondering if I had any business being there on that godawful hill, so obviously in the way.

Darcy — who has worked the Tour and the Giro, who has spent months in Europe shooting pro bike races — had fewer, if any, misgivings. All in a day's work to Darce. Not me; hey, I had misgivings.

So, after the race, I asked a couple of pro riders. They said the motors are always there, part of the racing. Sometimes in Europe the motors crash and take out riders; it happens. But the riders and the races would not get publicized without the photographers. The photographers couldn't get to the good shots without the motorcycles.

It's okay, Maynard, the pros said. It took two or three of them telling me, but eventually I believed. I'm pretty calm about it now. It was tougher to be cool on that hill there in New York. Yes, even for a seasoned cyclo-journalist like myself. Your man at the Trump Tour, just doing his job.

THE ATTITUDE

Thinking about the Tour got me thinking about how exceptional it is: The Tour de France is never considered by any racer — even by veteran pros — to be merely one more race in a long season.

Through the rest of the season, though, I've noticed that pro riders don't turn each race into a life-and-death saga. Here's what I mean.

Riding the BMW tech motorcycle in the Tour DuPont, mechanic Greg Miller and I follow Fabian Jecker (in second place) up Wintergreen mountain and across the finish line. Sky's black, thunder cracks, lightning forks down through the clouds. Spitting rain; soon it will pour.

Miller hops off, I park the motor, drag my yellow Mavic slicker out of the tank bag and walk back to the finish area.

A few riders have crossed the line, but most have not. The brutal, four-mile climb (seemed farther to me) blew the field apart. I stand maybe 10 yards past the line and watch one totally wasted racer after another pedal across.

Steve Hegg (Subaru-Montgomery), soaked with rain and sweat, rolls across the finish line. As he passes, he looks over and says, "Yo, Maynard. How're you doin'?"

Hegg's got the pro attitude. He takes his job seriously, but he doesn't *act* serious. He keeps a little distance. You begin to sense it if you're around these guys a while. The attitude.

Before each stage, guys would roll by, warming up. Some would stop a minute, say hi, maybe ask about the motor. "How do ya like that thing. Run good?" Or they'd ask if I liked working with Mavic mechanic Greg Miller as much as I'd liked carrying photographer Darcy Kiefel the previous few years. "Miller's not near as pretty," I'd say. Darcy, incidentally, was in Spain at that time, shooting the Vuelta for *Winning* magazine.

Or during races, riders would drop past us on the way back to their team car for water, or to chat. Or we'd have some occasion to pass up through the group. Amazingly, to me at least, guys would notice us there and say hi by name, "Hi Greg," or "Hi Maynard," as if they weren't 80 hilly miles into a hard day in the most important stage race in the U.S.

Perhaps you saw this one on TV: a rider who'd been fooling around for a TV camera fell and took down maybe 50 guys. No one suggested finding a rope and a cottonwood tree. Guys shrugged it off, even Nate Reiss, who broke his arm and had to abandon. Reiss turned his palms up: What can you do? "That's bike racing," guys said.

When we did wheel changes or helped racers who had problems, the guys we helped were always relaxed, cool. Miller would do the service, push the rider down the road. That was that. No high drama, no screaming. One guy calmly ate his food and watched the caravan go by while Miller laboriously unwrapped the cotton musette strap tangled in his rear axle.

Doing their jobs.... Those guys ride lots of races. The race organizers, announcers and press, also doing their jobs, will try to convince you that *this race today* is probably the most important, toughest, biggest-money race ever held.

But pros know, and so do "pro" amateurs, that (the Tour de France excepted) today's race is just another bike race, much like the one last week and the one they'll ride a week from now. Can't win all of 'em. The season's long. You pick your places or places pick you.

All these guys chose, obviously, to make their living (or at least devote a period of their lives) to racing the bike. Just as obviously, they have to love it. It can't be *just* a job, just a thing to do instead of trading securities, selling cars or delivering mail. Too hard.

But that commitment is a given among their peers. It goes without saying. And having to endure pain and frustration simply comes with their territory. Davis loses lots of sprints. Greg only wins a few races a year. Guys have bad days, or bad luck at bad times.

If you ride 150 races and win 10, you're a superstar. You lost over 90 percent of the time, but everyone wants your autograph.

Even though they are devoted to bike racing on the most intense level, mostly, when you see them, pros don't much want to talk about the race. And when you *do* hear them talk about races, the descriptions sound different from ones you hear on club rides.

You don't hear guys talking about how much they suffered; they seem outside of it. They describe running out of steam and having to slow down — without mentioning, as mortals would, the pain of "blowing up."

"It was fast," you might hear, "I could hang", or, "I couldn't."

They do what they can. Maybe it's enough at the time to get the job done, maybe it's not. They recover and do it again. You hear it all described, as I've suggested, as if they observed it, not lived it. Minimum drama.

We impose the drama, you and I. It's in *our* eyes, I believe, the eyes of us fans. To the racers, after dozens or hundreds of races, each one's a task, part of the job, just "bike racing."

I watched Erik Breukink calmly win the DuPont at the last minute in the Wilmington time trial. Breukink, just doing his job, pedaled (Beemer speedo) 42mph on flat sections, 25 up short hills, seemingly as calm as my mailman, who just delivered the latest *VeloNews*.

Their descriptions of their respective work days might sound somewhat alike, at least in tone. Two men at work. I'd rather watch Breukink. However nonchalantly he might describe his job, it looks awfully dramatic to me.

30MPH FOR 50KM

This interview with two of the 1992 world's gold-medal-winning team time trial women — Bunki Bankaitis-Davis and Jan Bolland — was conducted over dinner in The Small Wonder Café, a lovely restaurant in Boulder, Colorado, where both women live. We shared a quiet table inside the restaurant's Pearl Street-facing front window. Nice.

Interviewer and interviewees chose polenta baked with provolone cheese, spinach and marinara sauce. Each ordered a salad; the women specifying dressing on the side. The three shared a plate of mixed seafood stew. One extra-large dessert, persimmon pudding, proved adequate and delicious for three, accompanying lattes and house coffee. Hey, ya shoulda been there....

Q: Do you two use bicycle equipment made expressly for women?

Both: No. Definitely not.

Q: Is there an ethic among women racers not to use that stuff?

BBD: When I started racing, there wasn't much of it. When women's clothing came along, I don't believe the big team sponsors were involved. On a team, you get what the team gets — unisex clothing. Women's clothing wasn't offered to us.

We even ride the same seats as men. Because we spend hours and hours a day in the saddle, we can ride narrow racing seats, just like men do. But I can see, from having saddle discomfort after the off-season, that women who don't ride so much (or so often) might want something a little more padded.

JB: There're other things I wish manufacturers would consider ... like STI brake-shift levers. Women's hands are smaller; it'd be good to be able to reach them.

BBD: You know, these aren't necessarily gender differences — they're anatomical differences. Small-size stuff isn't just for women, but if it gets labeled "women's," guys won't buy it.

JB: Woman-specific products haven't made a big difference for us: We've adapted to what we've been given. Pieces of equipment, one thing or another, aren't all that important. We adapt.

Q: But you know people buy stuff 'cause they see you using it, as if you'd chosen it specifically.

BBD: Right. The real question is, if we were given the option of woman-specific clothing and equipment, would we opt for it? And we very well might.

For instance, on one team we got shorts that had a seam up the middle of the chamois. We complained and complained. We could ride another brand of woman's shorts for training, but we had to *race* in the uncomfortable ones. We were paid to wear them.

JB: Some sponsors — clothing sponsors with woman's lines especially — will accept your ideas and make special clothing for you: a pair of shorts, maybe.

Q: Will they put those shorts in their customer line?

Both: *No!*

BBD: They'll make 'em just for you and make 'em look like what they sell. I'm amazed more manufacturers don't use racer feedback to perfect their products. They don't, though, not from women racers. You never see the feedback turn into anything.

Some manufacturer has to take the risk, to design really figure-flattering clothing that works for women. To put two darts in a shirt and say: this is a women's line — I don't think that cuts it.

Q: Who made the bikes you rode at the world's? Who do they belong to?

Both: They're Yamaguchis, made for Performance. They belong to the federation.

BBD: We got 'em in April ... about time we got them on time. Then we went to a special camp in Colorado Springs. For a whole week, we did nothing but adapt the bikes to our positions. After that, there was no fiddling with the bike. We were ready to go, to concentrate 100 percent on training.

Q: How many training miles did the four of you do on those bikes, simulating race conditions?

JB: Do you think 1000?

BBD: I'd say more. We did two to three thousand total, but under exact racing conditions, maybe more like 1000. We had three camps....

JB: One in April, one in June, and one two weeks before the world's. At the world's, we rode together *all* the time.

BBD: The last two years, the TTT women have been a lot more team-oriented and unselfish. We had a common goal: to win gold medals. Not like a road race where, well, I might have to help this or that person. The mentality is different.

We had well-matched personalities. Everyone there wanted to be there, no question. Makes the coach's job easier, makes the racers' jobs easier. That was the biggest difference this year compared to past years.

Q: You'd go to the camps at Colorado Springs and just put your road bikes away?

JB: We'd take 'em. We'd train on our road bikes, too. Your muscles fatigue differently on the time trial bike, because it's a different geometry. You need to let your muscles stretch out — on your regular road bike.

BBD: And you'd be pushing a bigger gear on the TT bike: 54 chainring, 48-54, 12-18 or 19. And longer cranks.

Q: When you rode together, would you ride, say, 80 percent?

BBD: (Our coach) Hennie (Top) would give us five efforts that day, five minutes apiece, or three efforts at 15 minutes apiece. The shorter the effort, the greater the percentage. You could do 100 percent for five minutes, or until you blew...

JB: (*laughing*) Some people misinterpreted....

BBD: Right. Including Hennie. Sometimes we did 150 percent, as I recall.

JB: Every time you did an interval....

BBD: Oh my gosh. We were trying to get used to maintaining 30 mph. From the first camp, we started doing short intervals at 30 mph — race speed.

Of course, every time one of those sessions would start, you'd panic when the speed hit your legs. You could hardly hold on at 30 mph. It's just ridiculous.

Hennie would tow us up to speed behind the van, then accelerate away. We were supposed to do five minutes at 30 mph, then she'd come back and motorpace us until we recovered. Well, she was having us recover at what I believe was 40 mph.

JB: Yeah. She's a manhandler....

BBD: Shredded us completely. Maybe she was trying to see who was going to crack, who knows, but we had some really hard workouts.

Q: Speedometers on the bikes?

BBD: Yeah, to try and get used to 30 mph for the TTT distance, 50km. The workouts were designed to get your legs used to that speed, so everyone could maintain it, get to the front and not speed up or slow down.

Q: Did you stay a specific time at the front?

BBD: Hennie would say: "Do 30 seconds at the front." Sometimes if you felt like pulling longer that was okay, but sometimes she'd say: "30 seconds — that's it."

JB: She'd honk the horn to tell you to get off.

BBD: If it was windy, you couldn't do the whole 30 seconds. You had to know your strength and be honest about how you felt. You didn't want to pull 35 seconds — or feel bad if you could only pull 20.

JB: The object is just to keep the speed there.

Q: At the world's, was it your personal judgment how long you stayed at the front?

BBD: Yes. Hennie never honked. We had radio earpieces so she could talk to us — but Hennie's not a talker. By the time she did talk, toward the end, we were leading. The helicopter was hovering overhead. I couldn't hear a thing she said.

JB: My earpiece kept falling out; never realized it was gone. I couldn't hear anything, either. I was thinking, Hennie's not saying anything, we must be doing pretty bad.

BBD: The radio's good in training, but when it comes to the event, I mean, you're just like....

JB: Going as hard as you can go. You know when you need to get outa there.

Q: Did the four of you finish together at the world's?

Both: Yes.

Q: Do they take the time of the third finisher as the team's finishing time?

BBD: Yes, but we finished together. That was our other goal. We knew we could finish with four. Everyone equal; everyone riding so well. And no one needing to be a hero. We knew unless someone had the most atrocious day, even then she could hang on, we could finish with four.

JB: I don't even remember anyone missing a pull.

BBD: You know, last year in Germany, it was out and back on the autobahn. This year, I couldn't even count the turns....

JB: It was an especially technical course.

Q: Turns you had to shift down for?

BBD: We had to go into the small ring. We used the small ring the three times we climbed the finish hill. You could get bogged down terribly climbing that hill in the 54. I think we rode smart, doing that.

You couldn't just put your head down and ride that course. Maybe 20 of the 50km you could do that, but the rest was turns and off-ramps and on-ramps....

JB: The first 10km you could never establish a rhythm; too many sweeping turns, 90-degree turns with thick paint on the pavement....

BBD: Turns at the bottoms of hills....

JB: It took you through the beach area in Benidorm, a really touristy town. There were at least eight 90-degree turns in the first 10km.

BBD: It'd be some wide, screaming fast road that'd turn suddenly into a narrow street. And the roads *looked* so slick. The surface shimmered in the sun, looked like you were going to fall. After a while, we got confident on it.

JB: The Dutch riders said they'd been slipping. Depending on how you took the turns there were slick spots....

BBD: Probably the most technical course anyone could remember.

(The conversation wandered to Chip, Bunki's husband of seven years, then to Jan's four-year boyfriend, ex-bike racer Doug Tanner.)

JB: Doug was responsible for getting me involved with the sport. I'd been a rower at the University of New Hampshire.

BBD: I think if you look at top-level female cyclists, at least in the U.S., they've all been drawn into the sport by boyfriends.

Q: That's kinda controversial to say, you know. As in "behind every strong woman racer, there's a fine man...."

BBD: Men have given to us so unselfishly. I cannot tell you. Chip gave up any of his cycling ambitions, and said, "Bunki, if you're gonna go for it, *go*...."
Fact is, I've had very few close girlfriends. The close woman friends I've had have been like Jan, and Sally (Zack). I don't relate to the average girl. I don't want to go mall shopping. I don't want to put on makeup. I don't want to go to a bar.

I don't want to do those things. I would call up Jan and say, let's go ride 80 miles, let's ride to Estes Park (Colorado), let's do something physical. That's the way we *are*.

Q: Bunki, do you know how that's going to sound?

BBD: It'll sound terrible. Very sexist. Generally, I think, women are just wimps. Incredible wimps. You would never see me doing step-up aerobics. I wouldn't be caught dead. Never.

JB: We'd never go in the weight room with the little Lycra body suit things on.

BBD: To me, that defeminizes women. They think it's sexy. I don't know what they think it is. To me, it's just a pile of shit. They sit on that machine that makes their legs go up, down, up, down. Why don't they go to the mountain and haul their ass to the top and come down.

Q: Bunki, would you be proud to see this in print, even if it makes you sound like a woman-hater?

BBD: *Yes*, absolutely. When I raced in North Carolina and in Colorado ... we'd always do the men's races. I cannot tell you how wonderful, how protected I've felt in the pack, how....

JB: How encouraging the men have been....

BBD: Encouraging. If someone would bother you in the pack, some kind of ego problem, there'd always be someone there, right now, saying, hey, back off buddy. Always.

JB: Right.

BBD: I cannot say enough good things about almost all the male cyclists we've been around.

JB: The good male cyclists will want to encourage you, to respect you and your goals. It's the pack filler — those guys will give you a hard time about you being in the men's race.

Q: Because they're threatened somehow?

JB: Yeah. It's tough on their egos that we might be able to hang in a men's race. Early this year, we did a training race in Texas, a 90-mile circuit race in the Hill Country. We thought we'd ride half of it 'cause 90 was a lot of miles for the early season.

BBD: But our own egos wouldn't let us drop out.

JB: Erin Hartwell (Olympic bronze medalist in the kilometer time trial) said to us: I wanted to drop out so badly, but because you guys were still stayin' in there, I had to finish. I'da been outa there a long time ago.

BBD: You can probably print that, because we gave Erin so much heat about it. He's a great guy with a great sense of humor. He's never sure if we're serious or not. We could come up to him before a race and say: We're Gonna Kick your Ass. For a minute, he'd take it seriously.

There's always been this camaraderie between the men and the women. If you're having a bad day, if you're having a great day, there's always support. It's the most amazing thing.

Q: Why, then, do you think so many woman riders feel they don't get supported by men?

JB: Those women may not feel confident about their own ability. If you're lacking confidence within yourself, you're not going to be looking for it from elsewhere.

BBD: Exactly. Those same women won't do a men's training ride. They're afraid of failure. So many women are afraid of failure. Physically, cycling's a very demanding sport. You have to do a lot of homework before you do a men's race. Don't do one thinking, hey, I'll just sit in the back.

Don't. I get really mad when women don't take a men's race seriously. They do a women's race, then do the men's race afterwards and drop out after three laps. Makes a joke of the whole thing. If you do the men's race, do it to finish and do it to do well.

You can't be afraid to fail. You have to go on training rides with the men. You have to get dropped 10 times, maybe 20 times, maybe only one time. If you're persistent, if you know....

JB: If you have that drive, if you want to do it, you're gonna get over the barrier. I was petrified, last year when I moved to Boulder from New England. I didn't know how I was going to be able to climb; climbing's been a weakness.

I went on a group ride with some Coors Light guys. I didn't know how I'd do, I was kinda afraid. I did it and got over it. Rode fine. I had to give myself that much, say to myself, you can do it, you're strong, you can ride with these guys.

So what if you get dropped. They're guys and you're a woman and so what. You have to accept you might get dropped by them. You have to be willing to put it on the line. Your internal drive will make you get back out there and do it again. It's only gonna be to your benefit.

Q: If you could speak to the woman cyclists in the country, what would you say?

BBD: If you want to pursue cycling or any other thing, do it with your heart, not just with your ego, and not just because someone else tells you to. Everything you do has to come from your heart; if it does, you can overcome all the obstacles that're gonna be in your way.

Some of the obstacles are going to be physical, some emotional. I believe it's very healthy for women to overcome physical obstacles.

JB: To develop a more positive character.

BBD: I don't like to see women portrayed as physically incapable. Decide what you want to be and you can be those things. Women underestimate their physical abilities, their strength. An amazing transformation occurs when women realize that.

I wish everyone could do what he or she wants to do, not be confined by what parents or someone else thinks is right. I got my PhD and decided I was going to be a bike racer. Do you know how much grief I got for that?

Then, when you go to the Olympics, everyone's your best friend. You gotta say, hey, this is me and these are my terms. It's not easy to make yourself happy today. So many options...

BBD: Don't be afraid to fail. Never be afraid to do something because you might fail at it.

JB: Failing is only gonna make you better. Don't sit in the field. Go off the front; see how long you can stay. See what it takes to get you dropped, or to take you to the place where you're at the end of yourself; you can't do any more.

BBD: Do things you don't do well, things you feel uncomfortable doing. Physically uncomfortable, intellectually uncomfortable. Change. Otherwise you'll be stagnant all your life.

JB: Failure is a way to recognize where you're weak, what it's gonna take to make you better.

BBD: No one likes to fail. We were all in their same shoes; we failed, too. We just didn't tolerate it.

THREE-PERCENT MEN

Two of the pioneers of pro racing in North America are Bob Roll (who's finished more editions of Paris-Roubaix than any other American) and Alex Stieda (First rider from this continent to wear the Tour de France yellow jersey). I spoke with them a few years ago at a pre-season training camp.

Q: I've always thought there was something out of the ordinary about you guys — beside the smell of that cycling clothing over on the bed....

BR: You know, our group — me, Alex, Ron Kiefel, Andy, Greg, Davis, Chris Carmichael, Jeff Pierce — the things we've learned have not, until now, been a part of American cycling. We're the first guys from here to have had those experiences.

Like pioneers in reverse. We went back to Europe to reclaim something that was ours but had been lost. I think we have an obligation to tell people about those experiences. Sometimes I'd like to put it behind me, turn away; but cycling, the things we've done, will always be a part of my life.

Q: Well, guys, what's it like out there?

BR: There's no easy answer. Professional cycling has lots of different aspects. There's business, pure athletics, tactics....

AS: Politics....

BR: Politics ... mechanical ... it's this huge rotating orb of human experience. That's why it's so sweet. A good pro deals with all those aspects naturally. You can't force him.

You certainly can't force me to think like that, to be political. You can't tell me that if I don't do something, like talk to some particular person maybe, or if I say what I'm really thinking, I may not get a contract. A lot of pros can do that act. I can't; that part suffered in my career.

A guy might be brilliant technically, able to pedal very quickly. Or he might be very efficient or so strong he can muscle his way through races. Or able to be in the right place in the peloton at all times. Maybe he's so sly he can manipulate the team situation politically in his favor. If he has one or more of those skills, eventually he'll get a result and continue to get contracts.

The best pros do all those things well. Every pro does at least one of them really well.

AS: Really well.... The best managers recognize each rider's talents, bring them out and put them to use the best way. A guy like Mike Neel ... has a feel for people.

He won't even say anything. He can draw the best out of you and you won't know he's doing it. Sometimes it upsets people when he draws something out they didn't even know was there. And he has patience. Like Alcalá, for instance: Mike found Raúl Alcalá, took him out of Mexico, made him into a rider.

BR: And a contender for a Tour de France yellow jersey. Some directors take the worst aspect of a rider and make him think about that quality all the time. They think that'll make riders improve. Usually, they don't improve. They get a contract for the next year and ride even worse — then that's it. Back to the farm, the factory, wherever they came from.

Good directors are rare. Lots of them have come and gone even during my career. The best ones go on and on. Cyrille Guimard, Jan Raas, Peter Post — they've been around since they first picked up a bicycle. Hopefully, guys like Mike Neel won't get discouraged.

Mike feels strongly about what's cool and uncool businesswise, and he can be a little abrasive or distant in that regard. Hopefully, brilliant directors like him won't get discouraged because they lack brilliance in another way.... Racers, too.

Q: Tell me, Alex, about the "typical pro moment."

AS: In my mind, it's racing in Belgium, or anywhere, but Belgium comes to mind. It's pissin' rain, the wind's coming across the road at an angle....

BR: Slowed down by nothin' whatsoever....

AS: No trees ... no hills ... the wind's whipping across your face. Anything you say gets torn out of your mouth and thrown out into the cow shit. Cow shit's getting sprayed up at you off the road 'cause you're riding through where the manure spreader was the day before.

BR: It washes out onto the road. You have pig shit and cow and horse crap and human feces coming up *in your mouth* the whole race....

AS: ...from the spray from the rider in front of you. You look up; there's five echelons up the road. You look back; there's no echelon behind you. You're the last guy, just hanging on.

You can't pedal any harder. You pull on the bars harder, just trying to keep up. You're giving everything. You look up the road and there's a guy from your echelon attacking, trying to get to the next echelon. Nothing you can do. That's a typical pro experience....

Q: Bob?

BR: That freaking orange soup, man ... those freaking last month's carrots. To begin with, they grow those carrots in grey earth that's been overused for centuries. The carrots only grow a couple of inches long and pretty narrow. They boil them for a few hours.... This is all over Europe, you know....

AS: Not just France....

BR: No, not just France, but Belgium and Holland and Germany and Switzerland. Not Italy, because in Italy they have....

AS: They have a love relationship with food in Italy. Anywhere else it's more of an abusive relationship.

BR: No, the carrots don't grow very well. They boil them for a few hours. Then they serve 'em up. You can't eat them but they don't throw them away. They make soup out of them and freeze it. They've killed everything; any nutrient that ever snuck in there is long gone. And they serve it to you a couple years later. Everywhere you go it's the first course.

AS: It's a fact.

BR: So when you're suffering there in the gutter, eating cow shit, you're thinking, gee, maybe I'll get some orange soup this evening. What a bonus. That's all you can think about.

That's a typical pro experience. If you can't get used to that, you better stay home and go out to the Chart House and have a giant filet mignon every night ... for about the same price.

AS: Luckily, we weren't paying for that soup. The team paid for it. Ah, I guess we paid for it one way or another....

Q: So why would you continue to race, when you're helpless in the wind in that gutter in Belgium, guys are disappearing up the road, there's not a damn thing you can do, and all you have to look forward to is orange soup?

AS: One day ... one day, you're gonna feel on. And when you feel on, no one can beat you. Granted it doesn't happen very often anywhere and it happens a lot less often when you're racing in Europe, but.... It's almost addictive. You feel so good you'd give almost anything to feel that way again.

You don't get good form all the time ... but when it does hit.... You may not be able to win, but you become a factor in the race. If you ever do get the chance to win, well, that's the ultimate.

Why keep doing it? We kid ourselves that we might as well stay at home and beat our legs with a hammer. Might feel less pain. Hard to say why we do it....

I don't know.... I'm such a stubborn bonehead sometimes, maybe my German background, I get a challenge in front of me, I don't want to back out. I think, I gotta finish this thing, gotta go for it.

To me, when you're in a bike race, every human being in that race gets stripped down to their basic elements or instincts. Guys who quit races or can't cut it — they're not stubborn enough or tough enough or whatever you want to call that quality.

BR: Very difficult question. You ask yourself "why" so many times — what am I doin' here? Like Alex says, it's having the desire to be one of the best guys out there.

When you don't have form, you suffer in the gutter. When you don't eat right, sleep right, travel right and have the right equipment, you suffer in the gutter. Or on a climb or in the heat or the rain.

But when everything comes together, you fly. There's nothing like it. You're floating and no matter how hard you push on the pedals, it doesn't hurt. That's why you can hang; if you experience that once, you're going to try to get back to that place. When you're stomping ... that's what the Brits call it ... Yatesey [Sean Yates].

AS: *(fakes English accent)* Stomping form....

BR: Stomping form ... lotta guys will do anything to get that....

AS: And that means takin' drugs....

BR: That's when guys have trouble, getting into pharmaceuticals, narcotics, all that stuff. I'm content to race for the very rare times it comes naturally. And hopefully not jeopardize the rest of my life....

It's not cheating, you understand, so much as a desire to be on top of your game a little longer. They say you can never make a stallion out of a donkey. With drugs you can compress your potential as a human into a shorter span of time, speed up your metabolism, what have you, but it's gonna come out in the wash during the course of your life, so....

Ninety-seven percent of your year as a pro cyclist is abject agony, but three percent is pure ecstasy. That's what we are — three-percent men.

AS: Couldn'ta said it better. You know, I never planned to be a pro. Never planned to make a living at it, to win bike races so I could make mortgage payments. Never even dreamed of racing the Tour de France like some kids I've met do. Have some fun, do your best: that's what my folks told me and that's how I always approached it.

Becoming a pro just seemed like the logical next thing to do. I was loving doing the racing, traveling, meeting a lot of great people in the U.S. and Canada and Europe....

As the years went the pressure increased, not just to do your best, but to win at all costs. Cycling's a great sport until you reach a certain level. I've been thinking about that a lot 'cause Sam and I just had a baby daughter. What if she grows up and wants to be a bike racer? All that serious stuff, all that pressure....

Q: When did you two feel you were authentically part of the pro peloton? Was there a precise moment?

AS: I was thinking about that.... Halfway through the '86 Tour, in the Pyrénées, we were having coffee in the morning before the stage started. Somehow, off the bike, you get drawn to the guys you rode with on the climbs, guys at your level of strength.

Gerrie Knetemann was the most experienced of our group, the grand old gentleman. He'd ridden 11 Tours by then. I tried to absorb as much stuff from him as I could. As we drank our coffee it hit me suddenly: We're just getting ready to go to work. Like any guys getting ready to go in and punch a clock.

Knetemann said, as if he was speaking to me personally *(fakes Dutch accent)*: "We must be losing three minutes on the first climb. And on the descent, we'll be coming back two minutes because we'll be descending much faster than the leaders. So we're one minute back....

"Then on the next climb, it's harder, we must be losing five minutes. On the descent, we come back two minutes, that's four minutes. On the final climb, that's L'Alpe d'Huez, we must have 20 minutes for staying inside the time limit."

I thought, wow, cool, I'm in on it, he's giving me the scoop, 'cause he knows these climbs and this is it. This is real.

And the next spring in Amstel Gold.... I was on the rivet [on the nose of the saddle, thus going very hard — ed], in the pack on unfamiliar country roads. All of a sudden Knetemann said, "23, Stieda, in the 23!" Okay, I shift down and around the corner was this wall, and I'm ready for it because Knet's looking out for me. Cool. That's when I felt part of things, that I'd earned the respect because I was making the effort.

Funny, I was thinking about that only last week.

BR: I remember the Three Days of De Panne, one of the most miserable races on the calendar, right at the end of March in Belgium. Pure misery.

I was already exhausted from the season up till then. Wasn't April yet and I was wrecked, massacred. Wrung out. Like Swiss cheese on a rat trap put there three Christmases ago. That's what I felt like.

The last day we started fast on cobbles, in the rain, crosswind, pure misery. I had been falling three, four, maybe seven times a day. I just couldn't stay on the bike. Every time there'd be a movement in the pack, I'd [*whooshing sound*] be so exhausted, right over the bars.

The last day, we did all the climbs from the Tour of Flanders, the biggest race in the capital of cycling. Only Ron Kiefel and I were left from the team. I hate to drop out of a race. I probably should have 'cause I was seriously compromising the rest of the year. To finish dead last, you know....

I'd crashed three or four times just that day. I'd already taken every guy out — at least once. They hated me. Probably the only guy I hadn't crashed was Sean Kelly, 'cause he rode all the climbs at the front.

Hey, I would miss the descent completely, just go shearing off into five or six guys. Pretty soon they started looking back. If they'd seen me during the climb, they'd be nervous: "Where's that guy, that missile?"

Sure enough, on the last freakin' descent down the Kemmel, we had to veer to the left a little bit. Wham, I took out Kelly.

We went flying into this field. Just behind me was the wall of the town graveyard. Kelly says to me (*fakes high, squeaky Kelly voice*) "You take me out one more time, you're gonna end up in that cemetery, uh?" I looked up and said, "Screw you."

Kelly said, "You're gonna finish, then, aren't you?"

That's when I knew I was a pro.

AS: We don't realize how fortunate we were, how special the position we were in really was. It's great to have a forum like this interview to tell people what it's really like. Not a romantic dream like so many young people think.

They see the Olympics on TV and watch a couple of guys going hard and they think that's what it is. They don't realize what it takes to get to that level. They don't realize the sacrifices it takes: how many guys crashed, blew out knees, how many thrashed themselves and never made it....

BR: It's important to realize that what we get from cycling, what we got from riding the Tour, is not much different from what every person can get out of cycling. Going fast, enjoying the thrill of speed, feeling competent at what you do.... Everyone can enjoy that.

AS: You don't have to ride the Tour to get that feeling.

BR: Exactly. Everyone can go as hard as they can go in cycling. If you don't get to ride the Tour, don't get discouraged. That's not what it's about. You can enjoy cycling the exact same way we do and get the exact same pleasures we do from it.

ON THE
TRADE

STRADA MODEL

Anew year, a new decade … and a new bike. And not just any bike, one made-to-order, just for me. I'll walk you through its purchase and first weeks of use; you may find the process interesting. And you may want to find a builder like Tim Neenan and a bike like mine for yourself.

I never had bike problems in the past. I've ridden Italian production bicycles the last 10 years and found them delightful. I never thought I was a custom-bike kinda guy. I worried that I couldn't design one as well as the Italians I'd relied on all those years.

Then, last spring, I got to thinking I should have an American-made bike, built by someone I know and trust. That bike wouldn't need to be adaptable to the middle two-thirds of a bell-shaped curve of cyclists. It would be made for me. As my builder says, "We only build one size: your size."

The frame would distribute my weight properly over its length. It would account for my habit of pushing my butt off the back of the saddle on climbs. I could choose its lugs and crown and seat cluster, direct its cable routing. I could pick the paint and the parts. The bike would reflect my tastes.

Right away I thought of Tim Neenan, my friend since the late '70s. These days, Tim builds Lighthouse frames out of a workshop next to his home in the lovely Santa Ynez Valley, just inland from Santa Barbara, in central California.

Last spring, my wife, Shelly, and I visited Tim and Lorraine in Santa Ynez. While we were there, just for fun, he measured me and my bike, and drew a sketch of what *he'd* have me riding — when and if. Planting the seed, he was, and in fertile ground, evidently, because it sprouted. A month later, I sent him a deposit.

After he opened the deposit letter in March, pleased and surprised, Tim called, asking if Shelly and I could come down to Santa Ynez once more. We'd go for a ride or two and he could watch me on the bike. He'd remeasure me and my bicycle and make dead sure he was building me the just-right frame. We'll be down, I said — but it took until July before we were able to get to Tim's for my fitting.

We rode together twice, once flat, once hilly. Tim measured me again and taped and angle-gauged my bike. He told me what he thought I should have: a shallow seat-angle, a longish top-tube, such-and-such a head-angle and bottom-bracket height — all that stuff.

We decided my bike should be as Italian as could be; we'd be on known, hallowed ground there. I chose all Italian frame components: tubing, lugs, bracket shell, crown and tips. Shelly picked the color, a medium blue we figured we wouldn't get tired of. I paid the balance of my bill. I owned a future Lighthouse.

After the trade shows in October, Tim called and told me he'd just applied the last decals and the final clear coat. I should come down, he said; we'd put my bike together and go for a ride — my Lighthouse's first ride.

Shelly and I put the box of Campy Croce and Chorus parts in the car and drove to Santa Ynez, but I wasn't nervous. If she says I was, don't believe her. I don't know why she talks that way.

Need I tell you the frame was beautiful? Need I say that the paint was perfect, the details fussed-over? Should I say that, because of its deliberately Italianesque style, Tim called my bike the *Mod. Strada* — "road model" in Italian. It's there on the decal, on the chainstay.

We built the bike up in a couple of hours. He'd already installed the headset and bottom bracket, so the rest went right together. We mounted the virtually new, tied-and-soldered Spence Wolf wheels I'd been saving.

Tim built my fork with internal wiring for the Avocet computer. The wire runs inside the steerer, then out through the 3TTT stem. Only an inch of wire shows. Clean, clean. The whole bike looks sano, as hot-rod car guys used to say.

We finished the assembly and rolled out Tim's driveway for the ride, my bars still untaped — I *always* have to readjust my brake levers; I'm so fussy.

Any nervousness I might have felt was wasted. The new bike never felt strange. You'd think it would, new and different as it was.

For instance, I've never had so shallow a seat-angle. And I've probably never had precisely the same head-angle or fork rake or top-tube length. None of that even entered my consciousness. I worried for a while that the stem and bars and cranks were screwed on good and solid, but I never felt like I was on a new bike, out on its first ride.

That Lighthouse is, in its quiet way, by far the best bike I've ever owned. You're aware of how beautiful it is, but while you're riding, you never have to think about the bicycle. The quality of the bike and the builder's attention to its fit are reflected in what you do *not* notice.

It doesn't ride hard. It doesn't ride soft. It doesn't steer noticeably quickly, nor does it seem stable as a train. It just works. It feels planted, sure-footed. It goes wherever you want it, to the precise spot you want on the road.

It never needed a change of stem length or saddle height or fore-and-aft saddle placement. It disappears, as the road test cliché goes, under me. It's the best-looking, most undemanding, most responsive tool you could imagine. Worth the wait, worth the money, worth the worry.

When I walk into my garage, put on my cycling shoes and clump over to it, I imagine it thinks: Oh good, a ride.

I imagine it might say to me: Hi, I'm a Lighthouse Strada Model. I'll be your bike. Let's get out on the road.

COLD SETTING

"**B**ike Shop," Frank said, "this is Frank."

"Frank. How ya doin'? It's Andy."

"Fine, Andy. What's doin'?"

"Appreciate your answering the phone so late, Frank. Shop closed and all, I thought maybe you'd have a minute to talk to me," Andy said, "I got a problem."

"Best time to call," Frank said, "quiet here. What's on your mind?"

Andy said that since he'd gotten back into cycling, he'd been riding with the group from Frank's store. He liked those guys and he liked Frank; all the guys did. He said he tried to buy all the bike stuff he could from Frank.

"Thanks, Andy," Frank said.

"I want a new bike, is the thing," Andy explained. "And I want a Colossium frame like the Black Rebel team rides. I know I don't ride as well as those guys; I probably don't need a frame like theirs. But I want one. Anyway, I know you don't sell those frames. Like I said, I try to get everything I can from you. I didn't want to buy a bike somewhere else and have bad feelings between us, so I thought I'd buy the frame and bring it in. I'd buy all the stuff to set it up from you, and have you put it together. I didn't know how you'd feel about that, so I called."

"Hey, Andy," Frank said, "thanks for being straight with me. Couldn't have been an easy phone call to make, worrying about how I'd react.

"Listen, this isn't the first time I've thought about this. I can't sell everything, especially these days, with so much stuff on the market. Some items, like those frames, they only sell to one dealer in an area. I figured I didn't have much demand for 'em here, but maybe I misjudged.

"You know, it matters to me what you ride, because it reflects on me and the shop. I'd like to think that, whatever you ride, it works good for you and fits you right. If it's something I sell, that's great. But that doesn't matter nearly as much as knowing you feel free to come in or call and talk to me about things. Like tonight.

"Makes me feel I must be doing something right, that you'd call me about wanting some product I don't sell. Or maybe to tell me if you or one of the guys had a problem with something I sold, or with some work I did."

"Hey, Frank," Andy said, "guys don't have trouble with your work."

"Well, I do my best," Frank said, "but everybody makes a mistake now and then. You worry that you don't hear about the mistake, or the item you didn't stock, or something you sold that didn't work or didn't last.

"Too often, nobody says anything. You don't find out what you did wrong; you just lose the customer. Without a chance to correct what went wrong, or do the right thing, you lose a friend. That's *way* more serious than a guy like yourself riding Brand X."

Andy said he felt relieved Frank was so understanding about the frame. Meant a lot to him, he said. Frank asked Andy if he'd found a frameset somewhere, and already bought it or put a deposit on it. Andy said he had not. "Why don't I call the Colossium people tomorrow morning? Maybe they have a dealer near here they feel is doing a good job; maybe they don't. Maybe I can order one for you after all. Fifty-seven to the top, isn't it? If I can't, I'll let you know tomorrow. You can buy or order one wherever you would've; ask them the dimensions and get them to me. That way we can have everything ready to install. If you'll come by and tell me what you want in parts, and pick out some rims, I'll build your wheels first thing."

"Frank," Andy said, "I'm real pleased. I didn't want anyone else building my bike."

"Well, I'm pleased you called me tonight, getting this thing cleared away between us. Before you know it you'll have your new bike. You won't have to feel funny showing up on it at the store or anywhere. I expect you'll be riding it when you drop me on Reservoir Hill some Sunday morning."

"That'll take a while," Andy said, "but thanks, Frank. Hey, I appreciate your help. This bike's gonna work well."

"This is how things're supposed to work, Andy," Frank said.

A CIVILIZED COUNTRY

Bologna, Italy; Thursday, August 2, 1990: sidewalk cafe — latte #2....
Don't fret that I'm in Italy and you're not. We talked — at a meeting
before I left — about sending all you readers. Really we did. It was simply too
expensive. We decided we'd send me; I'd look around and tell you guys what I
see.

This morning, I see lots of commuter bikes, one-speeds mostly, ridden by every
kind of person. Traffic is insane here, but the bikes glide through the craziness,
parking in huge, cable-locked clumps, perfect for the narrow streets and alleys of
Italian cities.

Drivers even make room for cyclists, evidently considering them legitimate road
users. You hear very little horn-honking. I can't remember one screaming, gestur-
ing confrontation in two weeks. This is a civilized country.

In the cities you see lots of people on mountain bikes. Specialized, Klein and
Cannondale (at least) sell bikes here, and all the Italian factories produce "MTBs,"
primarily with Japanese components. I caught a Bottecchia mountain-bike ad on TV
yesterday.

In this style-obsessed country, one of the highest status items a young man can
possess is a mountain bike. To attain "way-coolness," he must wear American deck
shoes, a certain kind of quilted jacket or vest, from England, I think, and Ray-Ban
sunglasses. And he should spin around the piazza in the evenings on a Rockhopper,
or a Colnago, Rossin, Bottecchia or Cinelli MTB.

Ironically, a Rockhopper probably outclasses a Cinelli: It's American, you know.

The Italian component industry waited too long to take mountain bikes seriously, but the frame people jumped on the bandwagon a few years ago with some pretty
neat product. Domenico Garbelli of Rossin, the original bike sponsor of 7-Eleven,

was given a Ritchey by his friend Mike Neel, 7-Eleven's coach. Garbelli, who'd ridden cyclo-cross for years, immediately saw the appeal. He built the first Italo-MTBs.

But the parts guys, Campy primarily, started late and clumsily. Campy's trying. Valentino Campagnolo piled up the frequent-flyer points developing new MTB groups with the help of U.S. experts. Still, even in Italy, the Japanese have the MTB parts market sewn up.

And what a market it is. Walk into an Italian shop (in the north, for sure), expecting to see a mix of products like that of U.S. stores — and you'll be surprised. Except for one-speeds and kids' bikes, it's almost *all* MTBs.

So, then, besides racers, does anyone still ride skinny-tired bikes?

I saw *hundreds* of racing bikes last Sunday morning on the road between Milan and Lake Como — with old guys on 'em. Guys in their 40s, 50s, 60s, some even older, riding to the lake and back in ones and twos, and in packs.

All of them on Italian road bikes — hundreds of those guys — wearing club and pro jerseys and shorts, and not skinny. Chunky, in fact, but out there every Sunday I'll bet, up to the lake and back. As we drove they came at us endlessly, neat old dudes on Nuovo Record Colnagos, C-Record Rossins, Olmos and Bianchis, and dozens of names you've never heard. On bikes that seemed to fit 'em, too. Old guys looking good on their bikes.

Only one helmet per every hundred riders; cars and trucks screaming by. No problems. Was I hallucinating? Can a place so wonderful be real?

This morning, I'll bet, all over Italy, those same old guys are meeting for coffee. Each has a copy of *La Gazzetta dello Sport,* Italy's most popular sports paper, the pink-paged daily that sponsors the Giro d'Italia.

They're arguing in the most civilized manner about whether Greg "Lay-mon," as they say it, or the Soviet, Ekimov, will be fast enough to eclipse Italian cycling idol Francesco Moser's former hour record. I wish I were sitting there with those old guys.

I promise: I'm gonna listen to my Italian tapes, I'm gonna get fluent. Maybe I'll put on a few pounds. Next time I'm in Italy, I'll show up the first day at the café with my *La Gazzetta dello Sport.* I'm going to try to pass.

"Buon giorno. Caffe e latte, per favore." If it works, I'll be gone a while. Forward my mail.

ABSENT FRIENDS

In the late '70s, I foolishly thought I had real racing potential. The best equipment would help me fulfill that potential, I figured, so that's what I bought. My results continued to be mediocre, but my bikes ... wonderful.

Best of all was a Team Raleigh I bought in '78 or '79 from Sunshine Bikes in Fairfax, Marin County, California, where I worked. That Raleigh, one of the red, black and yellow ones, was a TI-Raleigh Racing Team replica. Gerrie Kneteman and Jan Raas each had one; so did a young NorCal amateur named Greg Lemond. And me.

My bike looked exactly like the ones the stars rode. It cost a fortune; I believe the only more expensive frame at the time was the U.S.-made titatium Teledyne Titan. Luckily, I worked at the shop and could pay for it out of a series of checks.

My Raleigh was made from the then-new 753 — the thin-walled steel tubing that builders had to qualify to buy from Reynolds. Bikies everywhere argued about the new alloy: it was stiff, it was limber, it was strong, it was fragile. They said you could only ride a 753 bike if you were skinny or weak or a time trial specialist. They said every damn thing.

I thought the light tubing gave that bike a lively, responsive ride. It felt nimble, like a light-footed thoroughbred on the road, especially when I rode on sew-up wheels and tires. I remember once, on a ride in Santa Cruz, a classy British racer and shop owner noticed I had clincher wheels and commented, "Clinchers and a 753: isn't done."

I loved that bike. I finished second in the Cat IV Berkeley Hills road race and generally did about as well as I've done on any bike I've owned. I was always proud of my Raleigh; they were rare and *so* good-looking. But I sold it.

Why? If I remember correctly, I convinced myself that the top tube was too long.

I thought I needed a short top tube to get the flat back and 90-degree bent arms I saw in pictures of European pros, like Didi Thurau. I probably figured the seat-angle was too shallow, too. Hey, I was well into my 30s, but I was certifiably stupid, so I sold it.

A doctor from Marin, Mike Mandel, bought it from me sometime in the early '80s. I always regretted selling it, though, and I'd think of it now and again, and sigh. Then, this summer, I got fitted for a new Lighthouse custom frame. My builder, Tim Neenan, calculated that I needed a relaxed seat-angle and a long top tube.

I remembered my red, black and yellow Raleigh and sighed again.

Ten years ago I had the right thing and sold it. So the next time I called Sunshine Bikes, I asked Martin Hansen there if he'd ever seen that old Raleigh of mine.

"The 753?" he asked. "Oh, it's here. The guy who bought it rides his mountain bike all the time now. The Raleigh's hanging in here on consignment. Why? You wanna buy it back?"

I went to Fairfax and took the bike down off the hook, and looked it over. Mandel had commuted from Marin to San Francisco through salty Bay fog; the bike looked lightly corroded. Chipped spots on the top tube showed rust. Some of the parts on the front brake had lost their plating and rusted badly.

On the other hand, the paint was all there and the decals looked pretty good. All the parts but the wheels were original. Originally my choices, that is: Those bikes were sold as frames only. You equipped them yourself.

I decided the old red rat looked all right. I wanted it, but I had a brand new Lighthouse coming — made to measure, angles and all. Why buy this one? On the off-chance, I borrowed a tape measure and an angle gauge from the shop at Sunshine. Sure enough, the old Raleigh dimensions and angles measured almost exactly the same as my custom frame would have. Maybe there *is* nothing new under the sun.

So I bought it back, lubed up all the (Nuovo Record) moving parts, touched up the paint, replaced the rusted brake pieces, and polished it up. Paradise is regained. That old bike still rides like it's alive, like a purebred. It's waiting for me now, out back, leaning against my garage, team paintwork glistening in the early-afternoon sun.

I don't believe it goes as fast with me on it now as it did then, a decade ago. I *do* know that, this time, if *I'm* not on it, it's not going anywhere. I guarantee it.

CODA

RANDOM ACTS

Adair Lara writes terrific twice-weekly columns in the *San Francisco Chronicle*. Recently, Lara wrote about her friend Anne Herbert who, in 1983, scribbled these words on a place mat in a Sausalito restaurant:

"Practice random acts of kindness and senseless acts of beauty."

Lara says Herbert calls herself a full-time worrier, that she "sees world history as a clash of hobbies." Here's Herbert's explanation. You should be able to figure out why I feel it belongs in a cycling hobbyist book:

"Each of us," Herbert says, "has something we just naturally like to do — making quilts, listening to sermons, shooting guns, creating model airplanes. We all tend to think the stuff we really like to do is way better than a hobby and in fact, something everyone should do."

Much like most cyclists.

Some people do evil acts, according to Herbert, trying to convert others to their hobby, the hobby "everyone should do." Even evil-doers, in their own minds, are "making the world better."

Instead of simply picking an activity and pursuing it, Herbert maintains, we become crusaders. If that's true — and I think it is — we should pick our hobbies carefully.

"My hobby," Herbert says, "is wondering how I could reduce the net cruelty in the world."

What an idea: reducing the net cruelty in the world. Quite a chore, huh? It'd take a ton of people and a ton of effort from each to make a microscopic dent in net global cruelty. But every little bit of anti-cruelty helps.

I'd like to suggest you set aside some small percentage of the energy you normally apply to your cycling hobby and donate it to Herbert's hobby. Apply a fraction of the money, sweat, time and persistence you invest in cycling or personal fitness to "reducing the net cruelty in the world."

How can you do that? I don't know that I can tell you how, the same way I can't tell you whom to vote for, or to work for, or whose records to buy. You can figure it out for yourself.

Try this: Imagine yourself practicing random acts of kindness.

Random acts of kindness. Say the words out loud. Do they bring to mind tender impulses nearly acted upon, gentle or generous deeds overdue, possibly never to be done? Sincere compliments unpaid, gratitude unexpressed, love unreturned, needy persons unheeded? You don't need me to finish this paragraph. Write your own list. Use the back of the page if you run out of room. Use Nevada.

I'm not suggesting you give up riding. Ride 10 hours ... and then spend one hour with someone really sick or really hurt or lonely. Don't plan it, don't pencil it in, don't expect anything. Make that act the most spontaneous of your day or week.

I'm not suggesting you deny yourself. *Buy* that exotic road bike. And afterward, go to your ATM, withdraw the equivalent of 10 percent of the money you paid for the bike, and use the money to make a difference, however fleeting, in someone's or a few someones' lives. Even if — if you sat and thought about it over a decaf latte — you might feel they haven't earned your help. Don't judge them. Help them.

Chances are the differences you make in their lives will live in your mind longer than will the difference the new bike makes in your time up Hero Hill. Perhaps not; help 'em anyway. Remember: net global cruelty.

Maybe after a while you'll get in the habit of committing those random acts of kindness: They'll no longer be all that random. To continue, you'll have to let your imagination run wild, conceiving ever more spontaneous caring acts. That'd be okay, wouldn't it?

I'm not trying to provoke you to cut short even one brutal workout or keep you from relentless pursuit of your all-time best kick-ass form. No way.

I'm just suggesting that Anne Herbert may have something here. Try her hobby, the practice of random acts of kindness, one-10th of the time you spend at yours, the practice of pursuing personal fitness.

After all, 10 hours of intervals, cross-training and gym work will make your legs heavy. One frivolous hour chipping away at world cruelty will put wings on your feet.

THANKS

In early May, I got a call from Elaine Greer, who works for the Safety Center of California in Sacramento, a chapter of the National Safety Council. Elaine asked me, media star that I am, if I'd appear at an awards ceremony June 8 at the Safety Center offices.

The Center would give prizes to kids, kindergarten through high school, who'd designed winning posters encouraging their peers to wear helmets when they ride bikes.

Unable to think of anything objectionable about that, I agreed to show up and suggested RAAM-winner Elaine Mariolle as a worthy cycling spokesperson who might also like to be there.

Weeks passed; I went to the Tour DuPont. In Virginia, while driving a motorcycle carrying a Mavic neutral-support mechanic, I suffered some kind of allergic reaction around my eyes. It passed and I thought I was home free. No way. Pneu-monia.

This morning, Elaine Greer called me again, just checkin' in. I told her about my illness and my fear that it wouldn't go away in time for the upcoming ceremony. Ms. Greer understood, recommending that I continue to rest and consume lots of fluids. The Safety Center and the kids would get along without me, sadly, somehow.

We got to chatting, Ms. Greer and I. She told me that she'd had experiences running this contest and preparing for the prize ceremony that had been interesting, dramatic even.

She mentioned that an eighth-grade girl from Newbury Park (near Thousand Oaks, in Ventura County, Southern California) had won her age-group prize with a wonderful poster. Said she'd gotten to know the girl a little and talked with her teachers and mom.

The girl, it seemed, came from a family that didn't have a lot — nothing extra, for sure. A mother raising three girls by herself. Ms. Greer told me that school-day lunches had been a problem in that household; the school had to help sometimes.

This daughter had been struggling for some years in Special Ed classes. It was just in the last year or so that she'd done well enough in mainstream classes so it looked like she could stay in them. I got the feeling that everyone liked this girl and wanted to help.

Well, as I said, she'd won first prize in her group in this statewide poster contest. Pretty big deal, *major* deal for an eighth-grader. But, as Ms. Greer explained, it didn't look like the little girl could make it to Sacramento to accept the prize, let alone be accompanied by her justifiably proud mom.

I said maybe there was something I could do. I told Ms. Greer I'd get back to her soon as possible and called a friend over in San Francisco. My friend, for whom the term "superguy" was created, does just fine in business. He typically does not have to worry about where the cash for his next banana-yogurt smoothie will come from. He lives well, rides and races his bike.

His secretary said he was not at his desk. I explained to her why I was calling. I explained about the girl from Newbury Park and her mom and the poster and all. I asked her to ask my friend to help.

I apologized for calling for a favor like that — I felt like I was probably the 112th person calling that morning for a favor — but she said she'd ask him and call me back. Sometimes, she said, he'll help, sometimes he won't.

Half-hour later she called back and said he'd help. I got a tremendous emotional rush, misted up. I thanked her profusely, probably embarrassed her. She took Elaine Greer's number in Sacramento; she'd handle it from there, she said.

Hour or so later, Elaine Greer called, said thank you, thank you, thank you. She'd booked the flights. She'd arrange transport for mother and daughter to and from LAX, and to and from Sacramento airport. Ms. Greer, I could sense through the phone, was thrilled.

As I thought about the ceremony, I got chills — hey, maybe from the pneumonia. I can't be there this Saturday, but the girl from Newbury Park and her mom will. Thanks Elaine Greer. Thanks again, my friend.

Sometimes, by God, things turn out just the way they should.